HISTORIC
TEXAS GYMS

HISTORIC
TEXAS GYMS

A TRIBUTE TO VANISHING TRADITIONS

JACKIE McBROOM

THE
History
PRESS

Published by The History Press
Charleston, SC
www.historypress.com

Front cover, top: Pretty much in the proverbial "middle of nowhere" is the hulking, sad and oddly stirring gym at McAdoo. While McAdoo has been a ghost town for decades, the gym is still there, and it's well worth a visit. McAdoo is about an hour southwest of Plainview, halfway between Ralls and Dickens just off Highway 82. *Photo courtesy of Randy James*; *bottom*: The wonderful old former African American school in Cleveland, Texas, is still beautifully maintained. It now plays host to youth leagues and little dribblers.
Back cover: The ruins of a wonderful old gym at Indian Creek. Located not far from Brownwood, this great gym has a magnificent mural still visible inside the eastern wall; *insert*: Unidentified middle school dance in an unknown Texas gym, sometime in the 1950s.

Unless otherwise noted, all images are courtesy of the author's collection.

First published 2019

Manufactured in the United States

ISBN 9781467141598

Library of Congress Control Number: 2019932642

Notice: The information in this book is true and complete to the best of our knowledge. It is offered without guarantee on the part of the author or The History Press. The author and The History Press disclaim all liability in connection with the use of this book.

This book is dedicated to my best friend and the love of my life, my wife, Sharen. Many years ago, she saw something in me that I did not see in myself and I owe everything to her. We've been together for some thirty-nine years, and she has always been supportive to any crazy idea I might have come up with. I want to be a coach…sure! I want to go to graduate school….OK. Aw, I just want to go back and teach again….Go for it. I want to write a book. Well, you know how that came out. So, for these reasons and so many more, I dedicate this book to Sharen Arnold.

And to the memory of my older brother, Frank (Mike),
and my younger brother, Robby.

CONTENTS

CONTENTS

PREFACE

Except for a few years overseas, I have lived my entire life in small towns in north central Texas, but my family has deep roots in the Texas panhandle. In fact, all four of my grandparents are buried in the somewhat oxymoronically named Happy Cemetery. If you don't know, there really is a Happy, Texas. Just head south out of Amarillo on U.S. 87, through Canyon (home of the Eagles and Raiders), and in seventeen minutes you'll be in Happy, home of the Happy Cowboys. My mom is a Happy Cowboy, class of '46.

A few months after my father (halfback, Canyon Eagles, '41–'43) passed away, I made my pilgrimage to the Happy Community Center for the annual McBroom family reunion.

Dad was the oldest of nine siblings, and it was a chance for me to see my uncles and aunts, all of whom were not getting any younger, either. There was my Uncle Johnny, a man who was wounded on the beaches at Normandy—twice—but never spoke of it. My Aunt Martha was there, too. Martha was career Army, and at one time she was the highest-ranking female NCO in the U.S. Army.

There were sounds of the rattling dominoes—"slapping them bones"— complete with so many laughs and lies; it was wonderful to be with those wonderful folks, most of them for the last time. Although unspoken, everyone there sorely missed their oldest brother, uncle and dad.

After that, my time was my own, so I started my melancholy meandering northwest to visit my oldest son and his family in Golden, Colorado. I was taking the "scenic route" out Highway 87/385 on my way to Clayton, New Mexico.

Twenty-four miles out of Dalhart, I saw an old, run-down brick building overtaken by thickets of brambles, weeds and poison ivy. I stopped and, stepping lightly and wary of rattlesnakes, I entered the doorway that changed everything. Of course, it was a gymnasium, long past her prime and very run-down. I could still see the remnants of bleachers, parts of the floor and even the ever-present stage in the old building. I could see where a play clock once hung and a faint outline where a mural of the no-doubt fierce mascot once loomed.

As I sat and daydreamed, I thought about this place. What was this school? Who were the kids who played here? What happened to them all? What are their stories? After a few minutes, I was sure I could hear squeaking sneakers, the thuds of bouncing balls and the shouts and laughter of those so many kids who romped up and down this floor so long ago.

Then, an idea began to form. As a basketball dad and former coach, I've been in many gymnasiums over the years. While some are forgettable, many more are impressive. What I particularly enjoy are old, historic and beautiful gyms that are still in use by schools and communities all across our great state.

I decided these memories need to be recorded. Once they're gone, they will be gone forever. Even worse, the memories of the kids who played there and the things that happened there that are important to the folks in that community will be gone forever, too.

But school districts across the state are faced with a very real dilemma. How do they maintain these wonderful, but often old, obsolete and decaying facilities? What if they spend, say, $1 million to upgrade the old gym? It would still be too small to hold regulation games. It would still be too hot much of the time. The locker rooms would still be too cramped, and today's students don't care to play in antique gyms; they prefer the new, modern glass and chrome rock-deafening monuments to excess that dominate our schools today.

These wonderful old gyms are clearly an endangered species. In addition to that, Texas once had more than three thousand independent school districts; today, there are fewer than one thousand. Today, hundreds of the old school districts (and their buildings) simply no longer exist. If you search, you may find a marker where an old school once stood or pieces of decaying foundation where a local can tell you about the old school. There are scores of decaying, hulking relics that are now homes to farm equipment, bats and

Perico gym.

their guano, rusted-out pickup trucks and an unbelievable treasure trove of absolute junk.

However, there are many more special (and often beautiful) small-town Texas gyms. These are our historic gyms of Texas.

That first gym is all that was left of Perico (pronounced Purr-ee-co) school district. After I left the Perico gym, the idea of this book was formed.

Faced with this daunting task, I had to make some decisions to hopefully limit the scope and focus of this book. To begin with, I decided to limit my research to the gyms in small Texas towns.

This book is not just about the gyms and memories of basketball or volleyball games. In small-town Texas, the gym was often the cultural or social hub of the community. If it was a Tuesday night in, say, Texline, most of the townsfolk might head to the gym to watch their beloved Tornadoes take on their rivals from Adrian. In addition, the gym hosted thousands of dances for thousands of kids. How many boys anxiously cajoled each other into asking that girl to dance? My palms still sweat just thinking about it!

The gym also hosted graduations, fundraisers, beauty pageants, talent shows, band concerts, school assemblies, pep rallies and so much more. After a tragic plane crash in 1959, the gym at Buffalo High School became a makeshift morgue. According to local legend, on a cold night in 1932 in

Above: Texline gym, home of the Tornadoes.

Right: Elvis Presley in the Gilmer gym, circa 1958.
Photo courtesy of James V. Roy and Scotty Moore.

the tiny east Texas town of Big Sandy (home of former Sooner great David Overstreet), the most infamous couple in America in their day, Bonnie and Clyde, stopped by the gym to take in some Wildcats basketball. Though Clyde's arm was in a sling, he and Bonnie socialized with the fans and even signed a few autographs! After a while, they left, and not one person who was there even considered calling local law enforcement.

Throughout the 1950s, young entertainers like Roy Orbison and Elvis cut their teeth doing concerts in gyms and auditoriums throughout the state. In south Texas, the gym hosted many a quinceañera.

Finally, the scope of this project is immense. I fully realize that I have surely missed and inadvertently left out many great and worthy gymnasiums across the state. For that, I truly apologize to any of you who may be annoyed by my omission. Rest assured, it was not intentional. I could only do what I could do, and this is what I came up with.

I hope you enjoy this book, and this journey, as much as I did researching and assembling it.

Aubrey, Texas, 2019

ACKNOWLEDGEMENTS

The most enjoyable and fulfilling aspect of writing this book was traveling around the state and meeting so many wonderful and helpful people. Texans deserve the reputation of being open, friendly people, and it was somewhat awe inspiring to meet so many awesome folks from all over our great state.

Finally, a book like this cannot be possible without the help and input from many people. There are certainly more than I've listed here, but I would be most remiss if I didn't thank the following folks:

My editors, Ben Gibson and Rick Delaney, Brian Brisco, Randy James, John Grigsby, Sharen Arnold, Karen Tibben McBroom, Emily Brisco McBroom, Dr. Jamie Wilson, Dr. Richard McCaslin, Dr. Ignacio Garcia, Dr. James Monaco, Michael Green, Jennifer Rhoades, Cindy Hunt McWhorter, Lance McWhorter, Bruce Yeager, Greg Ennis, Marty Hair, Christina Courson, Dr. Ronnie Gonzalez, Carl Robinson, Brit Webb, Jim Johnson, Howard Ballard, Sean Lemmon, Frederica Wyatt, Estanislando Martinez, Jay Myers, Beverly Olsen, Billy Espino, Joe Baker, Abe Gott, Billy Collins, Glen Nix, Gloria Martinez, Rene Aguillar, Rick Shrum, Kenneth Owen, Sam Goven, J.D. Stocks, Clyde Parsons, Billy Templeton, Dean Edwards, Carl Waits, Stoney Burkes, Pancho Garcia, Ben White, Mary Helen Vargas, Ray Matthews, Jo Allgood, Teresa Walker, Bob Lee, JoAnn Barnhart, Greg Gilbert, Syble Sparks, Donny Wiley, Doyle Russell, Hal Porter, Karen Kidde, James Ludwig, Bryan Hill, Landon Landry, Jackie Cleavenger, Shawn Reed, Kent Harris,

Ray Cogburn, Jim and Carolyn Shield, Charles Meek, Chuck Wyatt, Dr. Jim Parker, Patricia Cook, Jack Thomason, Teresa Battrick, B.J. Wyatt, Albert Armor, Carolyn Ballard, Gary Adams, Roy Gilbert, Karen Richter, Michael Holland, David Durham, Tish Klock, Lester King, David Lechler, Randy Hoyer, Debra Inkster, Cindee Reynolds, Ted Mahoney, Pat Hackworth, Rob Dwight, Walter Padgett, Linda Buffy, Harley Johnson, Ivan Goodwin, Ginger Burchfield, Dwayne Humble, Doris Gerron, Ginger Burchfield, Loraine Barnes, Kerry Cowart, Dr. Greg Poole, Kenneth Graham, Jim Meredith, Michael Hurd, Robert Brown, Jackie Carr, Collins Briggs, Bob Stringer, Troy Humphrey, Gary Oldham, Jaime Velasco, Leonard Kubiak, Michael Payne, Dr. Eddie Bland, Greg Ennis, C.D. Knoblock, Nick Olsen, David Rodriguez, Joe Bernal, Tom Lopez, Raul Zuniga, Ray Matthews, Kay Lard, Lynne Moore, Mary Ann Vaughn, Gina Rokas, William Reagan, Mike and Cindy Port, Cindy Jones, Lynn Hopkins, Ricardo Estrada, William Gorham, Jim & Suzanne Bardwell, Jo Allgood, Theresa Walker, Reece Blincoe, Scott Vincent, Judy Bishop, Donny Wiley, Doyle Russell, Hal Porter, Karen Kidde, R.B. Strain, Kyle McVay, Stoney Burkes, Armando Hernandez, Laurel Lamb, William Beauchamp, Michael Payne, Judy Williams, Dwayne Ross, Dr. Ignacio Salinas Jr., Shirlene Olson, David Sine, Charles Perkins, Bobby Templeton, Jay Baccus, Sean Leamon, Tommy Hall, Tish Klock, Sarah Roach, Donny Wiley, Rick Cohagan, Chris Wilde, Debbie Moreno, Beverly Olsen, Greg Enis, Gwenda Miranda, Jonan Eberlan, Tim Orsak, Patricia Cook, Kent Hargis, Doyle Russell, Ray Cogburn, Margaret Zurecky, Marc McDaniel, Maureen Lindsey, Patsy Yosten, Brenda Riggs, Kevin Sprinkles, Mary Eldredge, Dr. Kenneth English, Brian Hill, Marta Decker, Dr. Suzanne Wesson, Deitra Inkster, Dwayne Ross, Polly Boyd, Michael Smith, Linda Voight, Coy Holcombe, Bobby Templeton, Rickey Williams, Sean Leamon, Jay Baccus, Tommy Hall, Michael Caudill, Donnie Wiley, Bob Lee, Chris Wilde, Jackie Cleavenger, Jerry Pierce, Glen Hill, Jaimie Velasco, Bob Stringer, Gil-Rey Madrid, Amanda Urias, Lea Daggett, Jimmy Lipscomb, Mike Reed, Wendy Sanders, Barrett Hutchison and Larry McMurtry.

A WORD ABOUT THE WPA

The Work Progress Administration (WPA) was a very ambitious (and some said desperate) attempt by the U.S. federal government to create jobs for millions of struggling Americans on many different public projects, such as the construction of public buildings, roads and bridges. The WPA also offered jobs for musicians, artists and writers on art, drama and literary projects. However, for the sake of our discussion here, we will focus primarily on the construction of schools—especially gymnasiums—throughout the state. In the end, almost every community in the United States had a new park, bridge or school constructed by the agency.

The WPA was established in 1935 by an executive order of President Franklin Roosevelt. It provided work for citizens during the Great Depression, which essentially lasted from the stock market crash in 1929 throughout the 1930s. At its peak in 1938, these programs provided paying jobs for more than three million men and women.

Mired in the misery of the Great Depression, voters elected Roosevelt, then New York's governor, as their president in 1932. After being sworn in to office, Roosevelt quickly pushed a package of legislation, termed the "New Deal," through Congress to set up new federal agencies to funnel direct payments to suffering Americans. Most agencies were designed to provide work on government projects.

The WPA not only built traditional infrastructure projects like roads, bridges, schools, courthouses, hospitals, sidewalks, waterworks and post offices, but it also built museums, swimming pools, parks, community

The beautiful Moran gym and wall. A WPA project.

centers, playgrounds, coliseums, markets, fairgrounds, tennis courts, zoos, auditoriums, city halls—and gyms. Most of these projects are still in use today. In all, WPA projects built 5,900 new schools and gyms and 2,302 stadiums around the country.

Incredibly, this was all accomplished by largely unskilled laborers who were put to work under different New Deal initiatives, mostly WPA projects. Total expenditures on WPA projects through June 1941 totaled approximately $11.4 billion—the equivalent of $183 billion today.

Of all of Roosevelt's New Deal programs, the WPA is the most famous, because it affected the lives of so many people. Roosevelt's vision of a work-relief program employed more than 8.5 million people for an average salary of $41.57 a month.

Give a man a dole, and you save his body and destroy his spirit.
Give him a job and you save both body and spirit.
—Harry Hopkins, WPA director

UNDER THE DIRECTION OF Governor Miriam "Ma" Ferguson, Texas was very active in the WPA initiative throughout the 1930s, up until the outbreak of World War II. Prior to the WPA, crippling unemployment in Texas had been faced by Ferguson by persuading the state legislature to create the Texas Rehabilitation and Relief Commission in 1933 to coordinate the state's efforts with Roosevelt's relief plans. This enabled Texans to participate in various early New Deal programs, like construction.

While most of the workers available during this time were unskilled laborers, fortunately for us, there were also unemployed engineers and stone and brick masons, and beautiful examples of their artistry are spread all over this great state. One unique aspect of these projects is that, whenever possible, the construction crews used local materials. As a result, many gyms in the Hill Country were built with materials from the nearby limestone quarries. In north Texas, many facilities were constructed with the red sandstone so prevalent in the area. Almost every WPA gym is a unique work that stands alone, exclusively individual.

The WPA lasted until it was phased out in 1943, after it was rendered unnecessary by increased employment as the country geared up for what had to seem like an inevitable plunge into World War II. As the war approached, WPA projects became increasingly defense related, as workers built bases, runways and factories all over Texas.

Concluding that the national relief program was no longer needed, Roosevelt directed the Federal Works Administrator to end the WPA. In a letter of December 4, 1942, FDR wrote, "Seven years ago, I was convinced that providing useful work is superior to any and every kind of dole. Experience has amply justified this policy."

Roosevelt ordered a prompt end to all WPA projects, and with no funds budgeted for the next fiscal year, the WPA ceased to exist after June 30, 1943.

During its heyday in 1936, the WPA rolls had reached a total of more than 3,400,000 persons. Throughout its duration, the WPA built 651,087 miles of highways, roads and streets; it constructed, repaired or improved 124,031 bridges, 125,110 public buildings, 8,192 parks and 853 airport landing fields.

Under the WPA, hundreds of thousands of Texans were helped to provide subsistence for themselves and their families. Both sexes and all races were employed. WPA wages in Texas ranged from forty-five to seventy-five dollars per month. Peak employment under the Texas WPA program was 120,000 persons in February 1936.

In Texas, the WPA built and organized preschool play centers, playgrounds, community recreation centers, boys' clubs, girls' clubs and, during World War II, centers for all branches of armed forces personnel. All recreational programs were created with the idea of establishing permanent facilities.

WPA project plaque, circa 1937.

Although the WPA was not able to answer all the miseries brought on by the Great Depression, it went a long way toward bolstering the self-esteem of workers. A poem sent to Roosevelt in February 1936, in block print, reads, in part,

I THINK THAT WE SHALL NEVER SEE
A PRESIDENT LIKE UNTO THEE...
POEMS ARE MADE BY FOOLS LIKE ME,
BUT GOD, I THINK, MADE FRANKLIN D.

CHAPTER 1

PERICO

A FORGOTTEN GYM

Perico is on U.S. Highway 87, twenty-four miles northwest of Dalhart and eleven miles southeast of Texline in western Dallam County. The first recorded history of Perico was 1888 as a shipping point on the Fort Worth and Denver City Railway for the Farwell Park line camp of the famous XIT Ranch.

Several railroad section houses, a station built out of an old boxcar and a water tower marked the site throughout the XIT's heyday. The earliest population consisted of the section manager and his family, eight section hands and the station agent. In the early 1900s, Perico grew as a result of the W.P. Soash Land Company's promotional campaigns, and the post office was opened in November 1907. As the number of farms grew, the town became a center for supplies and education in the vicinity. The first school, a two-room concrete building, was replaced in 1924 by a larger complex, including a two-hundred-seat auditorium, teacher living quarters and, fortunately for us, a gymnasium.

> *Special Perico Entertainment*
> *Perico (Special)—Perico plans a rapid-fire program tomorrow night, said Principal Ed McMinn today. Everyone is invited. At 7:30 the Texline Tornadoes and our Perico cagers will start a double-header. Between halves or between games there will be an old-fashioned cake walk with, ten cakes as prizes. Cakes will be named "Man's Favorite," "Miss Perico," "Devils Dream," etc.*

This guy did not welcome visitors.

Added feature will be a school team of girls meeting members of the Women's Club in a cage tilt. Club members have been named "Chubby" Kennedy, "Skinny" Brewster, "Grandma" Harrell, "Postmistress" Timmermann, etc., McMinn said.

Dalhart Texan, *Saturday, December 12, 1936*

With such a small population, it was natural that townspeople often performed more than one job. Hugh Hamilton Sr. ran the Phillips 66 gas station and drove a school bus, and Mr. Timmerman was both storekeeper and postmaster. The town's other filling station was run by a man named Grady Edge.

The Perico school taught classes one through twelve, and total enrollment was estimated to be around fifty. Graduating classes were often just a pair of students. The school had four classrooms, an office and a basement. Warmth was provided by a coal-burning furnace that heated a boiler that sent steam up through the floor to the radiators. The school had the luxuries of indoor plumbing and interior staircases.

Christmas Dinner Held in Perico
Mrs. Walter LeCompte was hostess to the Perico Friendship Club and their
families Thursday night at a supper in the Perico gym. Everyone brought a
covered dish. Several members were absent on account of illness. There was
a Christmas tree. Gifts were exchanged, and games played. The table was
beautifully decorated and the supper delicious.

Dalhart Texan, *Thursday, December 26, 1957*

Another interesting aspect of Perico school was that it used what could be called "homemade" school buses. The bus drivers were also the town mechanics, so it wasn't considered much of a problem to build buses by using old automobile chassis. The school had three buses built in this manner. A wooden body similar to a camper shell was built and attached to the old frame. Seating was provided by three benches that ran the length of the bus. Heating was provided by running the bus's exhaust pipe up through the floor under the middle seat. The only entry and exit was through a single rear door.

The view from the baseline.

Odd things end up in old gyms.

The ever-present stage made the gym a multipurpose facility.

Hag-Stag Dance Tomorrow Night
The Huddle Club is entertaining a Hag-Stag Dance tomorrow night at the
Perico Gym. Dancing will begin at 8 p.m. The admission is 50 cents and
the idea is that all girls and boys will go "stag," and both girls and boys
pay admission; No dates are allowed. The whole student body is cordially
invited. "You will miss some fun if you don't come."
Mary Frances Arnold

Dalhart Texan, *Tuesday, February 8, 1944*

By 1931, the town had several businesses, including a general store, the ever-present west Texas grain elevator and a Foxworth-Galbraith Lumber Company. In 1947, Perico reported the school, three businesses and a population of thirty. In the 1960s, the population grew to forty, but as highway improvement drew away the town's trade throughout the 1970s and 1980s, Perico declined.

When the post office closed by 1970, the school was soon abandoned, and by the mid-1980s, the town had only one operating business, a grain elevator, and two known residents.

Perico gym, main entrance.

Perico, Texas, at one time was a small farming community with a country school, a gymnasium, a post office and a country store. The school closed around 1956 and was later demolished. Perico is now a ghost town on Highway 87, between Dalhart and Texline, Texas. There are still remains of some of the buildings, and the gymnasium is still standing. Late one night, as a friend of mine and I drove past Perico, I pulled off the highway and stopped the car on the dirt road in front of the gymnasium. As we stood outside the car, I remembered back more than fifty years ago, all the good times I had when going to school at Perico and how much fun all the students had roller-skating in the gym. We stood in silence for the next fifteen minutes.

Finally, I said, "Well it's late, we better get home." I opened the car door and then turned back for one last look. That was when a strange thing happened. In the distance I heard children's voices coming from that old deserted gymnasium. These were happy laughing voices. I did not say a word as we drove away from Perico and headed back to Amarillo. My friend, Linda, finally said, "Harry, who were those kids, and how did they know your name?" I did not want to admit to hearing a thing, so I said, "What kids?" Linda said, "The kids that kept asking you to stay with them." I had promised myself that I would not mention this story to anyone, but I am sixty-seven, and life is getting away from me, so I decided to share my story with you. Some lonely night, if you are ever driving past Perico, stop on the dirt road in front of the gym and listen for children's voices. They might invite you to stay.

—Ghost story submitted by Harry

CHAPTER 2

WHAT IF?

REMEMBERING THE TRAGEDY OF McCAULLEY

Twelve miles outside of Roby, where U.S. Highway 180 intersects with FM 611, the flashing red light was ignored and, in an instant, the town of McCaulley began to die. In the end, five students—four girls and a boy—were killed. Four were killed at the scene and another, Kathy Wilkerson, died in the hospital twenty days later. Seventeen kids were hospitalized, and the lives of everyone in McCaulley, Texas, were changed forever.

By all accounts, that morning of December 8, 1978, was uneventful in all respects. Every family member and friend has tales of irony to share. Kathy Claxton remembered arguing with her sister, Bonnie, over a blouse both girls wanted to wear. Bonnie was wearing that blouse when she died. Edd Farmer was the school superintendent, the basketball coach and the bus driver that day. At the end of the school year, Farmer left McCaulley forever. Some fifteen minutes after the bus left for the tournament, they had to turn around and go back because they had forgotten the water bottles. All told, maybe fifteen minutes were wasted, but the effects of the delay were catastrophic.

What if the team had not forgotten those water bottles?

What if, remembering the water bottles, they just continued on to the tournament in Hermleigh without them?

What if any number of things that may have delayed their departure one minute—or five seconds—had occurred?

Of course, none of that happened, and so the strangest, saddest and most tragic story of all Texas gymnasiums is the tale of the gym at McCaulley. It's the story of a school, its basketball teams and the town itself, as, incredibly, five members of the Eagles girls' and boys' basketball teams were killed on their way to a tournament. Their school bus was essentially sheared in half by a speeding oil well service truck driven by twenty-one-year-old William Dixon, who—incredibly—had already been drinking that morning. The heavy truck came rumbling down Farm Road 611 on a horrific collision course with the McCaulley kids. Witnesses testified that Dixon never even slowed. He did not have a commercial operator's license and was eventually cited for improper passing, failure to stop at a stop sign and failure to yield right-of-way.

As is the case in most small towns, everyone was affected. Small-town kids are everyone's kids. McCaulley school employee and resident Lorene Dowell remembers hearing that afternoon that there had been a terrible accident. "In a way," Dowell told Jeff Guinn of the *Fort Worth Star-Telegram* in 2005, "everyone else's child belonged to us, too.…They tried to notify all the parents of the kids on the bus, and, as they heard, they headed out to the location of the wreck."

Team member Earl Williams was injured in the wreck. "I don't remember anything really," Williams said. "I just remember being hit, and then there was blood everywhere."

Fisher County sheriff Mickey Counts said it was the worst wreck he had ever worked in his career in law enforcement. "They were thrown all over the inside of the bus," Counts said. "I don't see how any of them survived."

That was how Pete and Doris Pippin experienced every parent's worst nightmare. "At first, we heard one of our daughters was dead," Mr. Pippin said. "We didn't know which one." When he arrived at the crash site, bodies were lying beside the road, covered by blankets. "We were told by the police not to, but I had to know." That was how he learned his girl Bonnie was dead. Doris went with their younger daughter, Kathy, to the hospital in Snyder, where the girl could not talk for several days. In what was probably fortunate, Kathy remembered nothing of the accident.

The five deaths were about a tenth of the tiny high school's enrollment. There were three funerals in one day. Lorene Dowell recalled everyone in town attended all three funerals. "I cried until the muscles in my face hurt," she said. Indeed, if a community and a school can have a heart, the heart of the McCaulley Eagles was broken that day, and it never healed. It was the beginning of the end, for sure. Indeed, on that fateful day in 1978, for a town that may have already been on the ropes, that haymaker from Fate sent McCaulley to the canvas and set it down for good.

Close-up of the McCaulley gym.

Residents tried to carry on, but it was only a matter of time until there were no longer enough students to justify keeping the school open. "Times were already hard," Dowell said. "And when those children died everyone tried to support the high school teams, went to all the games. Afterward, with the memories of all those kids lingering, doing that just wasn't the same."

As was probably inevitable, ghost stories regarding the McCaulley gym began to surface. Rumors of late-night sneaker squeaks and bouncing balls began to surface after the school closed in 1987, when the kids had been dead for almost a decade. Vandalism is a constant nuisance to the caretakers of the property there. Windowpanes are shattered, doors are pried open and empty beer cans clutter the gym floor. Former resident Clint Powell told the *Star-Telegram*, "Lots of people, especially kids, know about the ghosts there. They're curious. They want to get in and see it for themselves." Powell did say that he thought the gym was haunted. A sister of one of the victims, Frederico Perales, said, "The souls of those dead kids still aren't at rest."

Anyone looking for ghosts doesn't have to look very hard. The harsh west Texas terrain seems to tell a story of its own. The Fisher County red clay is cotton country; it's hot and dry and dusty. Surrounding homes and business are all but gone. Yet, fittingly, the monolithic Eagle Gym stands out for miles around. It's easily visible from the cemetery where four of the five students

29

are laid to rest. Despite laudable efforts by locals who have, over the years, tried to preserve the old gym, the place is in a declining state of disrepair. Most of the upstairs windows are broken out. There always seems to be recently melted wax from "séance candles."

While locals may continue to struggle to keep their memories—and their gym—alive and maintained, things do not look good. "As my generation gets older, of course we're going to keep telling the stories," Powell says. "It's not going to stop."

The only positive aspect of that might be that the memories of those kids will not stop, either.

The students who were tragically killed as a result of the December 8, 1978 collision were Britt Jeffrey, Lolita Perales, Katherine and Rita Wilkerson and Bonnie Pippin.

CHAPTER 3

MR. AND MRS. FORT STOCKTON

T he folks who grow up and live in the Pecos County seat of Fort Stockton tend to be a hearty lot. The town pretty much survives on its own, way out in southwest Texas, a long way from anywhere. Being 330 miles northwest of San Antonio and 240 miles east of El Paso, Fort Stockton was originally an infantry outpost established as Camp Stockton in 1859. The primary purpose of the camp was to safeguard an excellent water source along the Great Comanche Trail on the Butterfield Overland Mail Route.

After a stint as a Confederate outpost during the Civil War, the camp was renamed Fort Stockton and became a permanent posting to the Ninth Calvary Regiment in 1867. The army remained in place there until it was abandoned in 1886.

The soldiers may have left, but the settlers of Fort Stockton remained and flourished. To a large degree, many of those settlers still have descendants living there today.

The Fort Stockton ISD probably came into being in 1908, although school, in some form or other, had been taught in the area for some thirty years. Classes were held in surrounding ranches before a one-room adobe building was set aside for a school in 1879. From that, Fort Stockton has continued to have fairly steady, albeit fluctuating, growth.

The wonderful Fort Stockton gym featured here was a WPA project constructed in the mid-1930s, and it was the home to many Panther and Prowler teams.

Above: Fort Stockton gym. A WPA project.

Left: Fort Stockton gym, east wall.

For those visiting the old gym, the trophy case still displays many awards and memorabilia, but what stands out is an old framed photo of an elderly couple known as "Mr. & Mrs. Fort Stockton," and this is their story.

Bill and Virginia Williams were married in 1936 in El Paso, where Bill was a manager of a Safeway store. In 1938, he transferred to open a Safeway in Fort Stockton. When the young couple moved, they were dismayed to learn that there were no rental properties in Fort Stockton at all. Finally, desperate for a place to stay, they dropped by the *Fort Stockton Pioneer*. The paper's editor, Shorty Sudduth, moved some furniture around in a room they "hardly used anyway," and the Williamses had a home. A short time later, they rented another room in town, where they had to share the bathroom with Clarence Wiley. Finally, they moved into the duplex owned by Tony Barone for twenty-five dollars a month.

Before the war, Bill took the civil service exam and went to work at the post office. Virginia was working part-time at J.D. Still Jewelry.

Like thousands of other men, Bill was drafted into the U.S. Army in 1943. After the war, he was offered a commission but declined. He said, "I'm a family man and I want to get home with my wife and my job." Finally, in 1950, Bill and Virginia moved into the new house they built on West Second Street, which is where they lived the rest of their lives together.

Another bas-relief is above the entryway.

In what was surely no coincidence, that house still stands across the street from the old gym. Billy Espino grew up, went to school and has lived his life in Fort Stockton. He was a teacher and a principal in the school and eventually served on the school board. "I remember growing up, before I was even in school, I'd go to see my friends play ball and the Williams were there. When I was in school and played ball, the Williams were at every game. Always." They were not just basketball and volleyball fans. Pick any football or baseball game, band or choir concerts, science fairs or track meets, and Bill and Virginia were there.

Virginia kept the "unofficial" book for the basketball games. After every game, the kids would come up to the couple in the bleachers, pore over their stats and discuss each game with their favorite fans.

"So, when I was in school and playing sports," Billy Espino continued, "Mr. and Mrs. Williams were there. They always sat in the same spot. The whole team would go up and look at the books and talk over the game. They were just wonderful people and we all knew they loved us."

Bill and Virginia Williams, Mr. and Mrs. Fort Stockton. *Photo courtesy of Gil-Rey Madrid.*

The final resting place of Mr. and Mrs. Fort Stockton.

It's worth noting that over the decades of following the Panthers and Prowlers, the Fort Stockton students' ethnicity profile drastically changed. While that may be true, the love and devotion Bill and Virginia shared for "their kids" never diminished.

Bill and Virginia also enjoyed travel. Over time, they ran through two RVs. Unsurprisingly, many of their travels allowed them to follow their beloved Panthers and Prowlers. For more than sixty years, the kids of Fort Stockton were always comforted to see them in the bleachers.

The Williamses received many awards: letter jackets, flowers and thousands of hugs from generations of Panthers and Prowlers over the years.

Bill and Virginia Williams continued to attend games until they were in their nineties.

Today, they lie side by side in Fort Stockton's East Hill Cemetery. Their shared marker is adorned by a Panther Paw, with the inscription: "GO BLUE."

Bill and Virginia Williams came to Fort Stockton to raise a family. In the end, while on one hand they may never have had any kids on their own, on the other hand, they had hundreds.

CHAPTER 4

TRAGEDY COMES TO TWO TEXAS GYMS

The gymnasium, like all school facilities, is part of a community. Besides school activities, local organizations often use the gym for meetings and fundraisers. However, because of tragic events, two small-town Texas gyms were called upon to serve under horrific circumstances. Because of those events, the perceptions and memories of those gyms were forever altered.

RANDOM SPRING THUNDERSTORMS ARE hardly a rare occurrence in Texas, but on one stormy spring evening, a flight scheduled to go from Houston to Dallas crashed into Margie Hill's pasture near Dawson, Texas. All eighty-four persons on board Braniff Flight 352 died on impact, and as emergency workers and law enforcement officers hauled bodies into the makeshift morgue in the Dawson Bulldog gym, the folks in the small central Texas town had an experience that was, at once, horrific, but also somewhat gratifying, as the community pulled together to support rescue workers, soldiers and, eventually, frantic family members who arrived, desperately searching for the fate of their loved ones.

The four-engine turboprop was a blistering fireball as it plummeted to the ground, slamming to earth just before 5:00 p.m. in a pummeling thunderstorm. Scattered plane and body parts would be recovered from over a half-mile area. At that time, it marked Texas's worst air travel disaster.

Many citizens of Dawson vividly remember May 3, 1968. As horrific as the catastrophe was, many residents remember it proudly as soldiers and emergency crews worked around the clock in cruel conditions searching for survivors and recovering bodies. Townspeople brought food and coffee and sheets from home. Churches and the bank stayed open, offering any assistance and comfort to devastated family members swarming to the scene.

Help came from the Salvation Army, Corsicana Emergency Corps, Texas Department of Public Safety and ambulance workers from Corsicana, Waco, Hubbard and Mexia, as well as soldiers from Fort Hood.

Charles Renfro was mayor in 1968. "We opened the gym for them to bring the bodies in, and then it was total chaos. Everybody from nine states came down and interfered with the recuse people." Body parts were matched and assembled in the gym. When a body was completed and identifiable, it was taken to the funeral home across the street. On the second and third days, it only got worse in the gym, which did not have air conditioning. Morticians and workers smoked cigars to mask the odor of decay.

The only body that was not horribly mangled was that of a soldier who had been killed in Vietnam. His body was being shipped home and was protected in his coffin.

Renfro said the town recovered, but the volunteers and rescue workers and the people who worked at the gym were "affected."

Once filled with echoing cheers of pep rallies and basketball games, the Bulldog gym still remains, pretty much unchanged since 1968, right on main street in downtown Dawson.

> *When I was about 5–6 my parents moved into a house next to the old brick gym where they put all the bodies from the plane crash years ago. Let's just say we have all experienced spirits in the house. I always heard screaming and voices in the hallways, and my doors would open or close on their own. I never slept right because when I was asleep the room would get real cold, and I'd feel something next to me in my bed. When I turned around I'd see the outline of a little girl or something as old as I was at the time. Ever since I can't stop wondering, what happened in that house? I wish I could find out for myself but people live in the house now.*
> —*submitted by Jackie, from the book* Dawson, Texas, Ghost Sightings

BUFFALO, TEXAS, WAS THRUST into the national headlines on September 29, 1959, when Braniff Flight 542 was only twenty-three minutes into a brief hop from Houston to Dallas, then on to New York. The Lockheed turboprop Electra had only been in service for eight days.

In 2009, local rancher Evan Moore told Vanessa Goodwin of *Leon County Today* that the debris started out about a half mile from U.S. Highway 75 on "the Ruben Long place. It was beyond Maurice Hester's place, toward Flo. 'Bout a mile past the first creek." The area was typical east Texas: sandy soil and tall pines. Flight 542 smashed to the ground in a sweet potato field.

Bodies of the twenty-eight passengers and six crew were strewn all about. Local men went immediately to assist, but it was quickly obvious that that was not going to happen. Officials from the Federal Aviation Administration (FAA) arrived and took over the scene, and the work of identifying the bodies began in earnest.

Before dawn the next day, local law enforcement from across the state had started moving the remains to the Buffalo High School gym, which was set up as a temporary morgue.

The *Buffalo Press* reported that "the local ladies set up facilities for serving sandwiches, coffee and cake at the school and were serving relatives and friends of the victims and the officers."

Of course, late September is still quite warm in Texas, and the week following the crash, Evan Moore remembers the gym as "kinda fouled up." His son, Leon, remembers that the gym still smelled of formaldehyde when they held their junior/senior prom there the following spring. Eventually, Braniff did pay for renovations to the gym at a later date.

The old gym was eventually demolished, and all that's left to remember Braniff Flight 542 is a plaque out on the highway on the outskirts of town.

CHAPTER 5

AUNT CORA FINDS A HOME

Of all the gymnasiums throughout the state, surely none are situated in a more beautiful, pastoral setting than the Clinger Gym, located in the heart of the Texas School for the Deaf in Austin. About twelve blocks down Congress Avenue from the state capitol, this picturesque campus is just across the Colorado River. Built in 1923, Clinger Gym is a classic example of aesthetic grace and understatement. Almost hidden among the two-hundred-year-old oak trees, the place still looks like there could be a game tonight.

Once inside, an interesting feature is the basement that runs the entire length underneath the gym. When wandering around the underground labyrinth of locker rooms, showers and offices, a visitor will, no doubt, stumble upon all that remains of a fantastic two-lane bowling alley. Although it clearly hasn't been used by students in many years, it's still extremely impressive.

This beautiful place was dedicated to former student "Aunt" Cora Clinger in 1983. Although she was a graduate of the school, that fact is only a small part of her story.

Cora Clinger was born on her family's farm near Llano on July 17, 1890. A high fever from meningitis left her deaf when she was just a toddler. Her parents first realized some symptoms when little Cora failed to notice the loud bell her mother would ring to call the hands to their noonday meal. She was admitted to what was then called the State Deaf and Dumb Institute on October 25, 1899, when she was nine years old.

Entryway to the beautiful circa 1923 Clinger gym.

Beautiful, hand-painted tile work adorns the gym.

When she was just fourteen, Cora was a star of the school's first girls' basketball team.

In addition to basketball, Cora also loved gymnastics, hiking and biking. During her senior year, she was named president of the Christian Endeavor Society. Although she graduated in 1913 with her class of eight—five boys and three girls—that really only begins her story.

Right away, Cora was hired by her alma mater and appointed "supervisoress" for the girls, and for the next forty years, she served as a "houseparent," supervisor, teacher, counselor/advisor and friend for hundreds of girls and boys who came to the school often scared and homesick. Her first job was overseeing the "big girls" (i.e., high school girls) in Dormitory Number 4. Her supervisors regarded Cora as an exemplary role model, a young woman who "exert(s) a good and elevating influence over the young girls." But the students knew her counseling and advice were based on her own personal experiences, common sense and genuine love.

Even after she retired, Aunt Cora continued to log more than five thousand hours as a volunteer at the Center for the Deaf at Austin State Hospital. She also retained an active role in the Les Sourdes Study Club, the Texas Association for the Deaf and the National Association of the Deaf.

At its 100th anniversary celebration, the Texas School for the Deaf dedicated the old gym to "Miss Cora Clinger, Benefactor, Friend, and Aunt to Hundreds of Deaf People in Texas." The gym is now known as the Cora Clinger Recreation Center in memory of the beloved Aunt Cora.

Certainly, there has never been a person loved by so many in the deaf community across the state of Texas as Miss Cora Clinger, whom practically every one of all ages affectionately called "Aunt Cora." During every homecoming or any major activity at TSD, alumni flocked around her just to greet her or engage in lively chats for the sake of "the good old days." As soon as people spotted her on campus, they…always made beelines toward her while excitedly signing: "Aunt!"
—*Jerry Hassell in "Profile of a Successful Alumna: Aunt Cora Clinger,"* Lone Star *(Spring 2002)*

CHAPTER 6

MEMORIES FROM A MEGARGEL HIGH SCHOOL MUSTANG

BY JAMO C. POWELL, COLONEL (RET.) U.S. ARMY

*This memory is presented here, in its entirety, from the Olney Enterprise *of April 9, 1998. Retired army colonel Jamo Powell is a Megargel Mustang (class of 1953).*

…One [landmark] had a very sizable impact on me and virtually every other Megargel Mustang for almost half a century. I toyed with the idea of writing about it, but kept putting it off. Then, a week or so ago, I happened to see a rerun of the movie *Hoosiers*. This is a movie about Basketball, folks—and I mean basketball with a capital B. Indiana takes its high school basketball very seriously and the movie did a great job of presenting the hard work, pain and, if you win, elation inherent to the game at that level.

So…reinforced by a strong dose of *Hoosiers*, has inspired me to write a few words about another important Megargel landmark—the Megargel High School Gym.

When I first came to Megargel in 1950, the gym was only a couple of years old. I have to admit, from the outside, it looked an awful lot like a big tin barn (and still does). But inside that barnlike exterior was the best looking and best playing basketball court for at least fifty miles in any direction. Pete Peterson, our wonderful coach, kept the floor polished to perfection and woe be to anyone careless enough to walk on it in street shoes. We were proud of our gym and when other teams came to play in it for the first time, they were obviously impressed. Most of them had to play in little crackerbox gyms where the out-of-bounds lines were so close to the walls you could barely find room to stand when you threw the ball in-bounds. Yes, we were truly blessed.

About 1950 Megargel stopped playing football. With our small student body, it was just too difficult to field a competitive eleven-man football team. In recent years the Mustangs have returned to the gridiron via the 6-man football route. I don't remember that being an option in the early '50s. At any rate, in the absence of football, basketball became our primary sports interest (for both boys and girls) and we spent a great deal of our spare time in the gym "shooting baskets." (Megargel schools closed in 2007. They were consolidated with Olney ISD.)

Even during the summer and on weekends you would usually find a few cars or pickups parked outside the gym and a "pick-up" game going on inside. All of this extracurricular practice, plus the fact that, without football, we could start practicing basketball seriously as soon as school started resulted in some pretty successful seasons in the early '50s. Indeed, just like the kids in the *Hoosiers* movie, we experienced a taste of elation a few times ourselves. Most notable of which was regularly beating Woodson (a particular nemesis of ours) and winning District one year.

Let me hasten to add here that I was not one of our better players. But even as a "sub," I took away some very rewarding and lasting memories of Megargel High School basketball, my coach and teammates, and our gym when I graduated in 1953.

Megargel gym today, from a distance.

We always had outstanding support from our families and other Megargel residents; the gym was filled to capacity at every home game. Without question the gym was the center of community activity and spirit during basketball season. When you consider that literally thousands of students and local residents have made use of this building since its erection, you begin to realize just how important it has been to Megargel. I have no idea what the future holds for this grand old gym, but I hope it will continue to be around for a long time to serve the needs of the school and community.

Every five years, I return to Megargel for our High School Reunion. It is really a great day for all of us—former students, parents and our own children and grandchildren. We include five graduating classes in our particular reunion. For example, the classes of 1950 thru 1955. Since our classes were so small (average size about 16 or 17), everybody knows everybody else at the reunion. I imagine we all dread the day a little bit, wondering how well others will think we've held up over the past five years. But, once there, that's all forgotten. It's almost like going back in time as we see classmates and rekindle old friendships once again.

One thing I always do sometime during that day is wander off toward that old tin barn of a gym. I go inside and just stand there for a while

Megargel gym, from the back.

thinking about other days. I notice that a lot of other reunion attendees do also. It still looks pretty much the same inside. It's got glass backboards now and the paint scheme is a little different, but the floor is still polished brightly and looks as good as it did nearly 50 years ago. And I still take off my shoes before I shoot a basket or two because even after so many years, I certainly wouldn't want Coach Peterson (now deceased) to catch me with my shoes on.

June 2002, Sarasota, Florida
© Jamo C. Powell
Originally published in the *Olney Enterprise*, April 9, 1998.

CHAPTER 7

MARFA, TEXAS

TWO GYMS FOR THE PRICE OF ONE

The old high school gym in Marfa is situated on a neat little hill, right next to the football stadium. The adobe fortress was a WPA project and was granted landmark status by the state in 2010. In fact, Hunter Gym in Marfa is quite likely the only art deco WPA-constructed stucco gymnasium in the nation.

Across town (which translates to about a five-minute drive) is what's left of Fort D.A. Russell. As was the case all over Texas, during World War II, the state was populated with several dozen military posts, all created to support the war effort. Fort Russell had a gym for the personnel stationed there, and it surely would be another broken relic by now had it not been for the extraordinary vision of legendary artist Thomas Judd.

MARFA HUNTER GYM

The venerable Hunter Gymnasium in Marfa is one of the most magnificent facilities anywhere. Named for the beloved former coach, Bodie Hunter, who coached both basketball and football there in the 1940s and '50s, the old gym still looks like it could withstand a siege from all comers. After 1945, Coach Hunter led the Shorthorns to six consecutive state basketball tournament appearances. Besides that, the 'Horns never lost a football game to the hated Fightin' Bucks from Alpine throughout his tenure.

The Hunter gym today.

Hunter gym.

The WPA project began in November 1940 and was completed in the spring of 1942. The contract was awarded to the architectural firm Frazer and Benner out of El Paso for the total fee of $1,000. The firm is also credited for designing the First Presbyterian Church, the Marfa Manufacturing Building and the Greyhound bus station in Marfa.

Longtime resident, historian and local Marfa architect Mike Green is a big fan of the Hunter Gym. According to Mike during an interview, like most WPA projects, the Hunter Gym was built with local materials. Adobe was selected for the exterior; the structure was truly ahead of its time. Even when applying today's LEED (Leadership in Energy and Environmental Design) certification guidelines, Hunter Gym would receive credit for its innovative design and use of regional materials. And man, could that place get noisy. According to local lore, when the concrete grandstand was packed, the commotion could be heard out on Highway 90.

In a final testament to its greatness, local residents say that, in the event of a large-scale disaster like a tornado, townspeople all know that the Hunter Gym is the place to go for safety. Think of it: in the event of a natural disaster, the safest building in town is still the seventy-seven-year-old gym.

But as with so many other old gyms, the school no longer uses it. A few years ago, a new gym was built. Nowadays, Hunter Gym is mostly used for storage. Nevertheless, it's impossible to see it without stopping to contemplate the greatness. It's magnificent, and the sight of it stirs our memory to think of bygone days. Sometimes, visitors can no doubt hear the echoes of Coach Hunter's whistle, pushing his team on to yet another championship season.

The gymnasium at old Fort Russell is now called "The Arena." It was built in 1936 for the soldiers stationed there. After the war, the fort was abandoned to the citizens of Marfa.

Fort D.A. Russell (originally called Camp Marfa) was established as a cavalry outpost in 1911. The open grasslands and the railroad made the site perfect for settlement. There were some fourteen outposts along the route for a significant military presence in the region. The famous matchups of cat-and-mouse between Mexican bandit Pancho Villa and U.S. Army general John "Blackjack" Pershing ran all through this wild and untamed territory. The sovereignty of the U.S./Mexico border was often ignored during these heated pursuits.

In 1933, the U.S. Cavalry at Fort D.A. Russell was discontinued, and the ceremony that marked the First Cavalry's dismissal of its horses was an emotional event. Nearly sixty years later, inspired by the story of Louie, the last cavalry horse, Claes Oldenburg and Coosje van Bruggen created a large-scale outdoor work titled *Monument to the Last Horse*. The piece honors Louie, who died on the fort and was buried on the site. It can be found just to the west of The Arena.

Toward the end of World War II, an American artist, Private First Class Donald Judd, probably got his first look at the magnificent open spaces of the Big Bend country from a troop train on his way through the Texas southwest. Years later, when he struggled to envision ideal ways to show his room-sized works of art, he recalled the wide-open spaces of Texas. He said he wanted his art to be a visceral, physical experience, and nowhere is this more evident than at The Arena. His work is clear, strong and definite. He believed his work should not represent anything. It should absolutely stand on its own and simply exist.

Mission accomplished.

A temporary suspension of operations at the base in January 1933 signaled a severe loss for Marfa, reflecting an equally difficult economic crisis across the country. Regular parades and sporting events such as polo, baseball and basketball were an important aspect of social life not only on the fort but for the civilian community as well.

Donald Judd's "The Arena." The old gym never looked better. *Photo provided courtesy of Randy James.*

Donald Judd's "The Arena." North entrance. *Photo provided courtesy of Randy James.*

By April 1936, Fort Russell reopened. Funded through the Works Progress Administration, the large gymnasium was built in 1938 using parts of a roof taken from an old airplane hangar. This building was wide enough to allow for social gatherings and festivities.

The end of World War II consequently led to the end of Fort Russell. In 1949, the government sold the property and returned the donated land to the city of Marfa. The gymnasium temporarily became a riding hall, and the rest of the buildings became increasingly more dilapidated. Fortunately, in 1977, Judd moved to Marfa, purchased some 340 acres and dedicated himself to bringing his vision to fruition.

After years of work and support from a few different foundations, the Chinati Foundation opened to the public in 1986. Today, it remains an independent, nonprofit institution. It was Judd's goal at Chinati to bring art, architecture and nature together, and his brilliance makes this "old gym"— The Arena—truly a work of art.

CHAPTER 8

BARRIO BALL IN THE CHICKEN COOP

H aving grown up in north Texas in the 1960s, I was familiar with the quest and struggle for school integration and the fight to provide a quality education for all Texas schoolchildren. However, my knowledge was limited to the plight of African Americans, and I was totally ignorant of the fact that Mexican American students in Texas experienced these same insults and anything-but-equal treatment.

In the 1930s, most Mexican and Mexican American students attended "Mexican Schools." These schools were usually poorly built one- or two-room shacks. Most had no running water or indoor plumbing. Teachers, who no doubt were caring and dedicated people, were often unqualified and not certified to teach.

So, not surprisingly, more than twenty years before Coach Don Haskins and his talented Texas Western Miners rattled the national sports landscape by beating heralded Kentucky and coach Adolph Rupp, a San Antonio high school had a legendary coach of its own. Carson "Nemo" Herrera built a program of hardworking, blue-collar kids who out-worked, out-hustled and flat out beat all comers in the 1930s and '40s. Over a five-year span, the Voks (the nickname was short for "Vocational") won state twice and finished in the top three the other three years.

Before the Miners shattered the color barrier for intercollegiate basketball, Coach Herrera and his program entirely made up of Hispanic boys were busy shattering south Texas stereotypes of their own. Year in and year out, the Voks were never tall, but they were always very fast and

State champion Lanier Voks in the old Chicken Coop.

very well-coached, and they were excellent shooters, ball-handlers and defenders.

During this time, both the coach and the players were developing a rabid fan base that knew how to rock their small, cracker-box gymnasium, which reporters dubbed the "Chicken Coop." By the end of the 1930s, walking in the Chicken Coop could be an intimidating experience. The place was jammed to the rafters with insane fans. By all accounts, the Chicken Coop was intense, involved and loud! Dr. Ignacio Garcia teaches (and writes) at Brigham Young University and is a Lanier Vok alum. In his terrific book *When Mexicans Could Play Ball: Basketball, Race, and Identity in San Antonio, 1928–1945*, Dr. Garcia writes, "It was always packed to the rafters with vociferous students whose cheering took the form of one deafening loud voice. Mingled in were whistling, booing and jeering."

However, by all accounts, the Chicken Coop crowd may have been intimidating, but never outside the rules. School administrators were known to be the harshest in the city.

Of course, Lanier High was not a rural school like those in the other stories in this book. However, the neighborhood surrounding the school, was, in every sense, a small town itself, and that made Lanier a small-town school. Most Lanierites lived in an area known as the San Antonio West Side. It was a "town within a city," wrote historian Robert Garcia. This area was often called "the Latin Quarter" or "Mexican Town" and, later, "el Barrio."

By 1943, Lanier's gym had become even more intimidating. A key aspect of their home-court advantage, at every home game, was that the Voks played with complete confidence. Their fans expected a win regardless of the opponent, and they used to fill their lungs to capacity all through the game. When opposing teams walked in, they usually did so tight and scared. The

Mexican opposing players felt particularly uncomfortable. Most, though not all, belonged to more affluent families and had not grown up in the barrio.

White players facing Lanier probably felt uncomfortable or isolated, since rarely did any fans from their school come to see them play at the Lanier gym. Most whites in San Antonio feared or at least felt out of place going to the West Side and coming into a gym jam-packed with Mexicans.

And who could not pull for a team whose players had such wonderful nicknames as "Goofus," "Indio," "Rough-House Kelly," "Chino," "Dracula," "Cockroach" and "Cupcake."

I could find no photos of the "Chicken Coop." It was torn down sometime long ago. I did find some yearbook photos of great players inside the old gym. Plus, we have some great descriptions. The former students I interviewed all had fond memories of the Chicken Coop.

For opposing teams, entering the Lanier gym was, most assuredly, an intimidating experience. It was a very small gym, with almost no out-of-bounds area. For every inbounds play, officials had to move fans out of the way, just enough to toss the ball in. Instead of the padding usually attached to the walls under the basket, the Chicken Coop had *colchones* (old mattresses) to serve that purpose.

Combine the compact confines and deafening crowds with lightning-fast, high-intensity defense, and it's easy to imagine what a significant home-court advantage the boys from Lanier must have enjoyed during their day.

The support—and safety—at home helped the teams to relax and just play ball. On the road, the Voks players and coach were subjected to every kind of prejudice. It was not unusual for the team to be refused service at

Legendary hall-of-fame coach Nemo Herrera.

restaurants. Hate speech laced with profanity was screamed in their faces. School or game officials could never be counted on to help; many of them felt the same way.

The most extreme example of this is recounted by Dr. Garcia. At an incident at an early 1940s tournament in San Marcos, Coach Herrera and his boys found themselves on the business end of a shotgun-toting bigot who asked why some "goddamn Mexicans" were attempting to enter a gym. When Herrera responded that this was his team, the racist replied that that couldn't possibly be true, because "everyone knew" that "Mexicans don't play basketball."

By 1939, the Voks were competitive every season, and when they were playing at Brackenridge High School for the city championship, Lanier alum Joe Bernal recalled a particularly tense incident. "Tony Cardona made the winning basket, and this guy ran up to him and smack! Hit Tony in the eye! That caused a big fight in the whole gymnasium." The rumble spilled out into the parking lot and continued until the San Antonio Police Department finally arrived.

Of course, that was more than seventy years ago. Certainly, the "old days" were not always "good ol' days" to many. And those attitudes may not be totally a thing of the past. In 2011, the Voks had another good team. They were mowing down their playoff opponents, and their next game was with Cedar Park High School in Austin. Shortly after tipoff, most Cedar Park students chanted, "USA! USA! USA!" This continued throughout the game.

Embarrassed Cedar Park administrators apologized the next day.

Coach Herrera taught his players the athletic creed of hard work, discipline and exemplary behavior both on and off the court with the promise that it would bring them benefits after their playing days were over. However, the treatment he and his team endured, no doubt, had a deep and defining effect on them all.

"You got used to it," says Bernal. "People were like 'goddamn Mexicans' or used bad language against us. Nemo was wise enough to tell us, 'Don't pay attention to them. They're just trying to get you. You just keep on playing your game and you'll beat them. That's the way to get even with them. Beat them!'"

And so, they did…frequently…and soundly.

Legendary coach Carson "Nemo" Herrera stepped into the Chicken Coop one last time in 1945. It was old, the floor was worn, some of the bleachers were overused and, if you listened carefully, he could almost hear the cheers, the boos and the quiet whispers that had echoed for the last seventeen years. Nemo was home.

CHAPTER 9

HEROES OF A SMALL-TOWN TEXAS GYM

Few veterans have a romantic remembrance of war. War is awful. When nations settle their differences by force of arms a million tragedies ensue. Nothing, not the valor for which it is fought, nor the nobility of the cause it serves, can glorify war. War is wretched beyond description, and only a fool or a fraud could sentimentalize its cruel reality.
—*John McCain, 1999*

It was a cold Friday night in February 1942, but inside the old gym at Ennis High School it was very warm—and rocking. Even though this was not one of the better teams the Lions had ever rolled out, it was always competitive, and the team played very hard. An excited crowd was nothing new; folks in Ennis loved all their sports and supported their beloved Lions. On this night, there was only a couple of seconds left in what had been an extremely hard-fought affair; the visiting Corsicana Tigers were always a tough matchup. The Tigers were up, 35–34, when Ennis coach Jude Smith used his last timeout. To be fair, most of his basketball team was composed of football players looking for something to do when it wasn't football season, and team captain James Wesley "Airedale" Goodwin was no exception. In the huddle, Coach Smith was drawing up what he hoped was the game-winning shot while the team listened intently. One of Airedale's best friends, Joe Crow, shared the huddle with his teammates, while his other best buddy, William Thomas "Dooney" Pierce, shouted encouragement from the bleachers just behind the bench. The team members then brought their hands together in the middle of the huddle. It's the same huddle break that almost all sports teams used then, as they still do today. "Lions!" the boys grumbled as they set up the play. What came as no surprise to anyone there, Coach Smith wanted the ball in the hands of his best player: Airedale. True to form, as the seconds ticked away, Airedale flashed his crossover dribble and slid to the hoop, where a collision ensued. The call could have gone either way, but, much to the outrage of the visitors, Goodwin was sent to the line. He calmly sunk both free throws, and the Lions sent their fans home happy, 36–35. That was remembered as one of the best nights in the old gym in Ennis. In a few short months, Airedale and Dooney would graduate in a ceremony in that same gym, and the three boys would become men… very quickly.

Show me a hero and I'll write you a tragedy.
—F. Scott Fitzgerald

THE THREE YOUNG MEN in the photograph are captured, forever young, hands together in their "all for one" handshake, excited to start their own grand adventure. These men—as well as Jack Lummus, another son of Ennis— are remembered here as true American heroes, and former Lions.

Some seventy years after the young men's deaths, their immediate families have dwindled to almost none. Ginger Boon, the youngest of eight children, is the last of the Crow family. Doris Mae Gerron, whose attempt to say "Junior" came out as "Dooney" and gave her brother a nickname he'd always carry, is the "baby of the family" and the last of the five Pierce kids. "Airedale" has one brother left, Bob, who lives in Georgetown.

Just before school started in 1938, Lee Crow, the new pharmacist at Hesser Drugs, moved his family from Milford to Ennis. They bought a white frame house with a big backyard only a block from the school, and they were soon overrun with school-aged kids eager to make friends. By the time school started, Lee's middle-school son, Joe Wiley, had met and would become lifelong best friends with two neighborhood boys, Airedale Goodwin and Dooney Pierce.

Joe was the third of eight children, and he was a year younger than Airedale and Dooney. Almost immediately, the boys were inseparable. By all accounts, all three were outstanding athletes in all sports. Probably the highlight of their athletic careers as Ennis Lions was the football victory on November 14, 1941, against the heavily favored Waco Tigers at Tiger

James "Airedale" Goodwin, Joe Wiley Crow and William "Dooney" Pierce. *Photo courtesy of Doris Mae Gerron.*

Stadium. Joe scored the winning touchdown in the game, which was regarded as the greatest Ennis Lion gridiron victory for decades to follow.

However, America was soon at war, and, like hundreds of thousands of American men, the boys were eager to serve. While Airedale and Dooney graduated at a ceremony at the old gym in the spring of 1942, Joe was supposed to return for his senior year. However, the friends decided that if they wanted to be together as much as possible, they all needed to enlist together. So, Joe skipped his senior year, and the three teammates and best friends were immediately ordered to active duty. After a farewell party hosted at the Pierce house (where the accompanying photograph was taken), the young men boarded a Pullman Company car on the Texas & Pacific Railroad out of Fort Worth and headed west to San Diego, and U.S. Marine Corps boot camp.

JAMES WESLEY GOODWIN

Airedale was the oldest of three sons born to Wesley Hiram and Ruby Ione Goodwin of Ennis. He was born on Friday, January 4, 1924. From a small boy, James was always known as "Airedale" because his wiry hair resembled the coat of an Airedale Terrier.

On December 7, 1941, when the Japanese attacked Pearl Harbor, Airedale was a senior at Ennis High School. He was an outstanding athlete, lettering in football, basketball and track. He graduated in May 1942.

Airedale enrolled at Texas A&M for the fall of 1942 but dropped out of school and enlisted in the U.S. Marine Corps with his buddies, Dooney Pierce and Joe Crow, for the duration of what was then called "the national emergency." Their strategy to stay together worked—to a point. After finishing boot camp together, they all volunteered to be marine paratroopers. After that, the boys were separated.

After extensive training for several months, Airedale's combat squadron was assigned to be "floating reserves" for the First Provisional Marine Brigade of the Third Amphibious Corps for the assault on Guam. Airedale Goodwin was getting closer to combat in the Pacific.

Finally, in February, Goodwin's unit joined a massive armada in Saipan. There, they were divided into three sections for the final leg to their ultimate destination: Iwo Jima.

JOE RILEY CROW

"Joe came home in '44," Boon said, "and I walked in the house—I was in the first grade—and he was sitting at the kitchen table with my mom," The visit was the last time Boon saw him.

Joe was expected to report for fall football practice in 1942 and enroll for classes at Ennis High School. But when he didn't show up, his coaches and teammates knew where he was.

The boys completed basic training together and volunteered as U.S. Marine paratroopers, which meant six more weeks of grueling training and jumps. They graduated—on time—and were awarded the coveted marine paratroopers' wings.

Airedale and Dooney received their next assignments, but Joe found himself hospitalized with a severe case of poison oak. As Dooney and Airedale boarded the train, Joe's orders were cancelled.

At the navy hospital, Joe was having a particularly tough time with a nasty case of poison oak. Navy doctors were unable to do much to relieve the discomfort and intense itching. But relief finally came in a package from Joe's dad, Lee Crow, the Ennis pharmacist. Lee mixed a salve that immediately stopped his son's allergic reaction, and the healing process began. Navy doctors were impressed by Lee's salve and asked him for the prescription.

After training maneuvers in the Solomon Islands and Guadalcanal, Joe had earned a thirty-day leave, so he went home for a last time. He returned to Camp Pendleton and there, in Hollywood, Corporal Joe Riley Crow married his high school sweetheart, Doris Rae Stephens of Ennis.

Returning to his unit after his leave, Joe was promoted to sergeant while on maneuvers with the First Provisional Marine Brigade until the maneuvers were called off and Sergeant Crow and his men received orders to proceed to Guam and then on to an island Joe had never even heard of: Iwo Jima.

WILLIAM THOMAS "DOONEY" PIERCE

Dooney was the fourth of five children born to William Thomas and Alice Christine Pierce of Ennis. His dad was a mechanic for the Texas & New Orleans Railroad, and Dooney was named for his father. From a very early age, everyone called him "Dooney," because his youngest sister, Doris Mae, could not pronounce "Junior." Since that moment, he was "Dooney."

Like his friends, Dooney was a very good athlete at Ennis High School, lettering in football and track. He graduated with Airedale and his fellow seniors at the old Ennis gym in May 1942.

For a while after graduation, Dooney went to work for the T&NO Railroad Company in Sherman, but he resigned to enlist in the U.S. Marine Corps in Dallas with his buddies Goodwin and Crow.

The boys wanted to stay together as much as possible, and for a while, their plan worked. They completed Marine basic training and paratrooper training together and on time.

However, after this, Joe got a bad case of poison oak. It seems likely that Airdale and Dooney never saw Joe again.

On Tuesday, October 3, the Joint Chiefs of Staff directed General Douglas MacArthur to assault Luzon on December 20 and Admiral Nimitz to assault Iwo Jima on January 20, 1945.

Dooney was assigned to Company C, First Battalion, under the command of Admiral Chester Nimitz. Early fighting in the Pacific was going well for the Allies, and Nimitz was quoted as saying, "Well, this will be easy. The Japanese will surrender Iwo Jima without a fight." This was hardly the first (or last) time officers misread combat conditions in the west.

On Wednesday, December 20, Dooney was promoted to sergeant in the Marine Corps and leader of a mortar squad.

When reveille sounded over the loudspeaker systems at 4:30 a.m., Dooney would have instinctively hit the deck, making his way to the head for a last shower and shave aboard ship.

Just like Joe, Airedale and thousands of his fellow U.S. Marines, Dooney may have sat down to the traditional breakfast of steak and eggs on D-day. Or, like many, he may have just opted for coffee, cigarettes and conversation.

The main assault force arrived off the coast of Iwo Jima at 6:00 a.m. Dooney sighted the island at 6:25 a.m.

At 6:45 a.m., orders barked, "land the landing forces." Dooney climbed over the gunwale and dropped to the deck to wait with others in his unit.

JACK LUMMUS

Although he probably never met Joe, Airedale or Dooney, Marine Lieutenant Jack Lummus, a former Ennis Lion, is very much a part of this story. Jack was ten years older than the other young men and a college graduate. By all accounts, Jack Lummus was a remarkable man in every respect.

Born on a cotton farm in southeast Ellis County on October 22, 1915, Jack was the youngest child and only son of four children born to Laura Francis and Andrew Jackson Lummus; he was named for his father.

Jack attended Ennis High School from 1931 through 1934, excelling at athletics in football, basketball, baseball and track. He was a tall, lean and muscular young man with great hands and speed.

After a stint at Texas Military College in Terrell, Jack received an athletic scholarship to be a Baylor Bear. During his four years at Baylor, Jack was a rare two-sport athlete and was All-Southwest Conference and All-American in both baseball and football. At the time, many considered him to be the greatest center fielder in school history, and he most certainly could have played major-league baseball. However, Jack was drafted by the New York Giants to play football and was an immediate starter at tight end. In his rookie season, the Giants made it all the way to the NFL championship game before losing to the Chicago Bears.

Baylor Bear and New York Giant hall-of-famer Jack Lummus. Jack was, arguably, the greatest athlete to ever come out of Baylor. He could have played major-league baseball as well. Former Bear baseball teammate Travis Nelson said, "Jack could cover more ground than a six-inch snowstorm." *Photo courtesy of Jacklummus.com.*

Then, like so many other men at the time, after the Japanese attack on Pearl Harbor on December 7, 1941, Jack walked away from his NFL contract to join the U.S. Marine Corps.

So, on January 30, 1942, Jack joined thirteen other recruits and boarded a Pullman car for his journey to San Diego, California, and basic training.

After boot camp, Jack was sent to the Marine Corps Officer's Candidate School in Quantico, Virginia, where he graduated 36th in a class of 255. After graduation, Lieutenant Lummus volunteered to join the Marine Raiders, an elite fighting group within the elite fighting group that is the U.S. Marine Corps.

During his training to be a Raider, Jack was promoted to first lieutenant. Upon completion of his training, he was granted leave to go home to Ennis for a few days to see his family.

After his leave, Lieutenant Lummus was officially detached to the Fifth Marine Division at Camp Pendleton.

When on liberty for a weekend, Jack met Ethlyn "Skipper" Bookwalter on a blind date, and it was a perfect match. The two made plans to be married after the war, if only…

Medal of Honor winner Jack Lummus. This mural adorns the hallways of Jack Lummus Intermediate School in Ennis ISD.

For Jack and Skipper, it was love at first sight. Skipper later wrote that they had an understanding. "And I understood how he felt—from the very beginning—I guess we just about always understood each other....From the day I met him I loved him."

Upon receiving orders to proceed to what everyone knew was war in the Pacific, Jack called Skipper at her office to say, "Goodbye, for a while."

He also telephoned his mother and sisters, Thelma and Sue, to say he was shipping out. At 8:35 a.m. on August 12, he sent a telegram to his sister Thelma to tell her he would write when allowed. "Give love to mother and rest. Love, Jack."

On October 3, 1944, First Lieutenant Jack Lummus and his fellow Marines left California for Iwo Jima.

IWO JIMA IS A tiny volcanic island in the Pacific Ocean about seven hundred miles south of Tokyo. The highest point of the island is Mount Suribachi (elevation 554 feet) on the southern tip. It is four and a half miles long and two and a half miles wide. Other than that, the island is described as flat and featureless. The island was particularly significant to the Americans for the airfields situated there.

The Japanese military began a massive buildup on the island, preparing for what they considered to be an inevitable invasion by the United States. All civilians on the island were evacuated, and none ever returned. On February 19, 1945, the U.S. Marines attacked, and the horrific campaign raged for more than a month, effectively ending on March 26. The beaches that were preferred for landing were rocky and mostly inaccessible, so, essentially, the only place for the U.S. Marines to land was along the east beach.

The Japanese 109th Infantry Division was under the command of Lieutenant General Tadamichi Kuribayashi, who was considered a tactical genius. The garrison had months to prepare a near-impenetrable fortress of underground caves, bunkers and hospitals, as well as an enormous cache of food, water and ammunition some thirty to fifty feet underground. These were all connected by sixteen miles of tunnels and manned by 21,000 well-trained army and navy troops who had taken a blood oath to die for their emperor. In the end, more than 19,000 of them died; only about 1,000 were taken as prisoners, 2 of whom did not surrender until 1951!

The Americans countered with three U.S. Marine divisions, some 70,000 men. Before landing commenced, the U.S. Navy pounded Japanese defenses for an incredible seventy-four days. However, unaware of Kuribayashi's tunnel defense system, many of the Americans assumed the majority of the members of the Japanese garrison were killed by the constant bombing raids. Incredibly, in the end, the bombardment reportedly had little effect on the Japanese defenses there.

Headed for this insane human meat grinder were the four young men from Ennis.

THE BATTLE FOR Iwo Jima raged for weeks, with steep prices paid for each piece of sooty ground. Progress was measured by the bloody foot, but when a platoon scaled Mount Suribachi and raised the American flag in that famous picture by Associated Press photographer Joe Rosenthal, every marine's heart lifted a bit. "It's the most beautiful thing here," Airedale Goodwin wrote to his family.

On March 5, Airedale and Dooney managed a short visit for a time when Airedale Goodwin's battalion replaced Pierce's. It's impossible to know, but it's not a stretch to imagine that the two exhausted young marines sat together and talked about better days. Days like school dances in the old gym, or the great game in Waco, both of which must have seemed like eons ago, and in another world, to be sure.

The fighting remained as savage as ever. On March 7, on Airedale Goodwin's sixteenth consecutive day of hellish combat, he received orders to seize the rest of the island. While his unit was to be relieved in two days, Airedale never lived to see it. During a fierce exchange, Goodwin was shot in the abdomen, a wound that in World War II was fatal 70 percent of the time. Private First Class James Goodwin died on March 9, 1945. He was twenty-one.

At 12:45 p.m., the Third Battalion began landing on the right flank of Green One. Joe Crow's Company G landed in the middle of extreme artillery fire. One explosion was particularly close, and Joe was knocked to the ground, probably sustaining a concussion. However, he was the leader of a demolition squad; his men needed him. Somehow, he struggled to his feet and moved forward.

The first night on Iwo Jima was cold, sleepless and fatal to many. Japanese artillery and mortar fire rained down on the Americans during the night. For Joe and his demolition squad, progress was measured by one enemy pillbox at a time. Pillboxes were concrete and steel-reinforced structures barely visible above the surface of the island. They were protected by well-fortified rifle and machine-gun fire.

It was extremely treacherous.

Joe led his demolition squad through heavy fire toward their objectives, three heavily fortified pillboxes. He skillfully led his men into position and relentlessly destroyed two of the emplacements. Joe had just set a satchel charge at the third and turned to run back to his squad when a machine gun opened fire on him at point-blank range from a concealed position. Joe was hit twice in an arm and four times in the chest. He was twenty.

Sergeant Crow, a veteran of three landings, was posthumously awarded the Silver Star for heroism.

The first wave of attack commenced at 7:50 a.m., and Dooney Pierce was in that wave. He was a sergeant in charge of a mortar squad. Eventually, Dooney's Company C had advanced some 250 yards under withering fire.

The entire division line was in the open, in full view of the Japanese, and Dooney and his men dug in for the night. Darkness came to the island at 6:25 p.m.

Hartgrove Millersview. Located almost in the exact center of Texas, in Concho County, this is a WPA-era gymnasium that's been maintained by the residents and is being used today as a community center. *Photo courtesy of Randy James.*

The Navasota gym and surrounding wall is still beautiful today. The wall extends some two hundred yards and encircles Rattler Stadium. According to lifelong Rattler Jimmy Lipscomb, there was nothing better on a Friday night than walking down those stone steps from the home locker room in the old gym to the stadium below. Jimmy and his teammates can still vividly recall seeing their biggest rivals—the Brenham Cubs—impatiently pacing across the way.

Besides making ice cream, the residents at Brenham have built a beautiful stone gym of their own.

The WPA gym at Brookesmith was beautifully constructed by skilled architects, stonemasons and laborers during the Great Depression of the 1930s.

The magnificent Toyah gym was built in 1912. Toyah may have been quite a town in its day, but its biggest claim to fame is probably that aviator Amelia Earhart spent five days there while having some maintenance performed on her plane. *Photo courtesy of Randy James.*

How can a sixty-something Caucasian male dunk a basketball? Stand on a four-foot-tall pile of pigeon poop. This old gym is overflowing with the stuff. *Photo courtesy of Randy James.*

A hidden treasure of a gym is in tiny Duffau. The gym is in Erath County, not too far from Stephenville. *Photo courtesy of Randy James.*

View from the balcony in the remarkable Gordon gym.

The formidable WPA gym in Granger is still widely regarded as the safest building in town, regardless of age.

The magnificent ruins of the old gym in Indian Creek, long since deserted. *Photo courtesy of Randy James.*

The Adams gym in Lockhart.

This is a beautiful setting for the old gym at Mont Belvieu, formerly the Barbers Hill High School gym. When it was discovered, the town was situated on a substantial salt dome, and petrochemical companies invaded, buying up land that was ideal for petrochemical storage. After a "few explosions," in 1985, the Barbers Hill School District deserted the area, but this picturesque old gym remains.

The Tehuacana wooden gym is one of the prettiest gyms in Texas. It was built in the 1920s. The headmaster at nearby Westminster College reportedly "cajoled and harassed" a local lumberman to donate the lumber for the much-needed gym. Finally, the lumberman relented and donated "*one* wagonload of lumber" for the project. So, it was done, and witnesses verified that one wagonload, pulled by a team of four horses, stacked fifteen to twenty feet high, was just enough to complete the job.

A view from the cheap seats in the Slidell gym. Inside, championship teams from one of the most historic programs in Texas are remembered going back to great squads in the 1930s.

Inside the beautiful old gym at Richland Springs, a WPA project.

The Pettus gym.

Perico gym bleachers.

McCaulley gym today, northern view.

Bas-relief artwork above the ticket window at the Fort Stockton gym.

Hidden away in the basement of the Clinger gym is a long-forgotten two-lane bowling alley.

Ruins of the magnificent Scranton Academy school and gym.

The view from half-court inside the beautiful Moran gym.

The Waelder Wildcat remains on guard on the old gym wall.

Although currently used for storage, the old gym at Navasota will soon get a much-needed facelift. This is great news!

The old gym at Winters now serves as the Blizzards' weight room.

The folks at Cisco had a creative use for their old gym. They tore out all the bleachers and dressing rooms and made an indoor practice facility.

Evidently, the old gym once served as the bus barn for Noodle ISD.

Artwork on the floor of the gym at Little River, home of the Bumblebees.

The magnificent ruins of Mosheim School.

The façade of the old gym at Moselle is unique. Almost all Texans I met were warm and wonderful folks. The dubious owner of the gym at Moselle…not so much. Escorting me "off his damn property," he was shirtless, riding a four-wheeler, with a Budweiser in his drink holder and a deer rifle across his lap.

The old hangar-style gym at Nixon-Smiley.

View from the home bleachers inside the Gruver gym.

When the first mail call was made the next morning, Dooney borrowed a sheet of paper and pencil and wrote to his family and to his high school sweetheart, Betty. In the letter, he asked his mother to take the letter to Betty to read and to tell Airedale's girlfriend, Deanie, that he had not yet seen Airedale, and added, "The fighting has been so fast I have not had time to find out if he's all right or not."

Casualties continued to mount, and on Monday, March 5, General Harry Schmidt ordered a day of no attack for the Third, Fourth and Fifth Marine Divisions. Front line units were reorganized, replacements were assigned and letters were written.

On Tuesday, March 13, sunrise came at 6:21 a.m., and Dooney and his men were given the ominous order to seize the remainder of the island.

Casualties continued to mount, and it was during this advance that Dooney Pierce was killed.

Dooney was observing Japanese positions to find targets for his mortar squad when a bullet from a sniper's rifle struck him in the head; he died instantly. He was twenty.

On Friday, February 9, Jack wrote his sister Thelma:

> *Dearest Sis,*
> *It's been a long time since you heard from your long-legged brother....I needn't explain why I haven't written....Our outfit is aboard ship and going into combat—just where and when I can't say...don't get excited if there is a delay because I'll write the first chance I get when we are ashore. There will be lots of work to be done before we have everything secured and little time for writing....Take good care of yourself and say an extra prayer for your bud.*

On February 24, D plus 5, morale was lifted by the first mail call of the assault. Jack wrote a brief V-mail to his family:

> *Dearest Mom, Thelma and Sue,*
> *Just a few words of greeting...please don't worry about me—I'm O.K. and still full of vinegar. Will write again soon as I can—Love Jack*

Ironically, in the same assault that claimed Airedale Goodwin's life, Lieutenant Jack Lummus was leading his platoon against the heavily fortified Japanese pillbox positions. He took three of them by himself. By eyewitness accounts, Lummus was a man possessed. He would shove the

Final resting place for First Lieutenant Jack Lummus. The Congressional Medal of Honor is the highest honor bestowed by a grateful nation.

barrel of his carbine through the gun ports and fire in every direction before tossing in fragmentation grenades. Doing this, Jack was wounded, but he continued to shout, urging his men forward.

As his fellow marines poured around him, Lummus stepped on an anti-personnel mine. The horrific explosion ripped away most of his lower legs. According to documents from the battle, Jack rose up on what was left and never stopped shouting. "Don't stop now! Keep going!" he yelled, and his platoon pushed forward.

The sight and the encouraging words from a mortally wounded Lummus inspired his men, effecting a blending of rage of average men with normal emotions into possessed fighting men.

A navy corpsman quickly came to Jack's aid. Kneeling beside him, the corpsman worked rapidly to slow the bleeding. He started the first unit of plasma before Jack was lifted from the broken ground and placed on a stretcher.

When the stretcher with Jack passed the Second Battalion's command post, Major John Antonelli and his staff rose in awe of the man from Ennis. Jack was pale and in shock; death was near. He opened his eyes, pulled the doctor to him and said, "Well, Doc, the New York Giants lost a mighty good end today."

Indeed.

Jack Lummus died under the bright lights of an operating table near the east beach on Iwo Jima. He was twenty-nine.

On May 8, Major Antonelli wrote Jack's mother and sent a copy to Jack's fiancée, Ethlyn "Skipper" Bookwalter. The major wrote, "Jack suffered very little for he didn't live long. I saw Jack soon after he was hit. With calmness, serenity and complacency, Jack said, 'The New York Giants lost a good man.' We all lost a good man."

On the evening on Memorial Day, May 30, 1946, in a ceremony at Ennis, Texas, Jack's mother, Mrs. Laura Francis Lummus, received her son's Congressional Medal of Honor. It is a grateful nation's highest award.

THE BATTLE FOR Iwo Jima raged for thirty-six days and thirty-five nights.

The official casualty report totaled 21,872 marines and 2,728 navy personnel. Within these casualty numbers were the dead: 5,885 marines and 433 navy men. Furthermore, 46 marine and 448 navy casualties were listed as missing in action and presumed dead.

Lieutenant General Holland M. Smith, the top-ranking U.S. Marine at Iwo Jima, later said, "Iwo Jima was the most savage and the most costly battle in the history of the Marine Corps."

JACK, AIREDALE, JOE AND Dooney died a long time ago. Almost all the folks who watched them on the football field or in the old gym are gone, too. But it's so important we remember these men, forever young in our photographs and memories, as they were then.

In the end, these boys from Ennis may not have been much different from millions of others who fought and sometimes died for their country. They were loved and sorely missed. It's their friendship, and the way their lives ended on the same sad island, that makes their story special.

They wouldn't be separated in life and, in the end, they couldn't be separated in death.

MEMORIES OF THE ENNIS GYM

It is always sad when things from the past are replaced for the progress of the future. Even though the demolition of the old gym and stadium by the former junior high facility will be replaced with a new structure that is needed for the children in the community, the finality of the actions to remove it are still hard to watch.

The old gym, which still proudly displays the words "Home of the Fighting Lions," was a gathering place for many, a venue for date night for some and a constant source of weekly entertainment as local athletes performed for the cheering hometown crowd. The bleachers in the gym were great hiding places, and more than one athletically challenged soul found solace in hiding beneath them, avoiding the dreaded words, "Suit up!"

Equally, the stadium has had its fair share of special moments when championship footballs games were won, special musical numbers from the band were played and many community relationships were formed. For a

The Home of the Lions. Original art by Karen Tibben McBroom. The gym was razed in 2008.

close-knit community, those relationships are important, as for most; they have carried on through the years and remain today.

While some would argue that the buildings are merely wood, brick and glass or that the stadium is empty now and new things need to be built so a new generation can make memories, we choose to remember the old.

The truth is, buildings are simply the construction materials they are made from, but the life and experiences had in them allow them to take on a personality and become a beloved part of the community.

So as progress marches on, we hope the community will join us in sharing their memories of the past and keep a special place in their hearts for the events and buildings that have helped us be able to move on to create new memories today.

("Memories." *Ennis Daily News.* Ellis County Newspapers, Inc., July 3, 2008. Accessed September 9, 2016. http://www.ennisdailynews.com/editorials/archive-2632/.)

CHAPTER 10

ELVIS VISITS GYMS OF TEXAS

JC's Name Teams to Sell Hayride Advance Tickets
The Gladewater Junior Chamber of Commerce today named teams and captains in their ticket sales campaign for the Louisiana Hayride show which appears here Saturday night, April 30.

Chuck Miller, ticket chairman, said the JC's have approximately 2,500 tickets for sale. The show to appear here will make its regular Saturday night broadcast from the high school gymnasium in Gladewater. This is one of the few times which the Hayride has left its home base at Shreveport.

Admission prices are $1.00 for adults, $0.50 for children. Persons wishing to buy tickets may contact any of the following JC's listed below in teams:

—Gladewater Daily Mirror, *April 12, 1955*

I sorta got my start in Texas," Elvis Presley told reporters during a stopover at Dallas Love Field in August 1958.

While Elvis came from the dirt roads and beans and corn bread of Tupelo, Mississippi, musical experts agree that the frenetic and raw performances he spread all over Texas throughout the 1950s made him into "The King" most of the world came to know.

Stanley Oberst, author of *Elvis in Texas: The Undiscovered King, 1954–1958*, uses a 1955 Texas state road map to follow Presley's travels around the state. He says, "There should be an official Elvis route marked with signs—the 'Hound Dog Highway.'"

Among the hundreds of appearances Presley made in the 1950s, several gyms hosted the frenetic rocker and thousands of sweating, dancing and screaming fans enjoyed nights they would never forget.

From 1954 to 1958, Elvis, his band and often fellow musicians from the *Louisiana Hayride* performed at the gyms in Hawkins, DeKalb, Gladewater (twice) and Paris. At almost every stop, stories abound from the folks (mostly pretty young women) who encountered Presley on his tours. (The *Louisiana Hayride* was a traveling country and western musical variety show that came into prominence in the last days of radio in the late 1940s and lasted to the beginnings of television in 1960. The show was an extraordinary hit. Eventually, it was syndicated on the CBS radio network to 198 affiliates and even overseas on Armed Forces Radio. In addition to Elvis, the *Louisiana Hayride* was a vehicle to stardom for such legendary musical performers as Kitty Wells, Bob Wills and the Texas Playboys, Hank Williams, Jim Reeves, Johnny Cash, George Jones and Buck Owens.)

A great story is one of nineteen-year-old Elvis in 1954, when three intrepid seniors from the tiny east Texas town of Hawkins ventured to Shreveport with the hope of snaring a surefire moneymaker to raise the cash they needed to fund their senior trip to Panama City Beach. Previous attempts at fudge sales and the like had proven to be dismal failures.

The plan was to send a committee of three senior boys, led by super-salesman Doil Stone, to Shreveport, attend the *Hayride* and find a performer they could convince to come to Hawkins to raise money for the senior class trip. They found a guy they thought was perfect: Elvis was young, hip and within their budget. The young men sealed the deal with a handshake, and it was set: Elvis Presley was coming to the Hawkins, Texas high school gym.

There was still a major problem for the boys as they returned home. They had to get the permission of their school superintendent, the imperious and thoroughly intimidating Deacon Smith.

Either because the superintendent was unaware of who Elvis was at that time, or, more likely, the way the boys presented their clever and innocent pitch to the man in charge, the show was given a tenuous green light. Late Friday afternoon, December 17, 1954, a borrowed yellow Bellaire pulled into the Hawkins gym parking lot with a standup bass strapped to the roof. The guys in the band lugged their equipment into the gym and onto an impromptu two-foot stage, no doubt cobbled together by the boys out in the Ag shop.

All this time, basketball practice was going on, so the band worked around the players. Some forty minutes into practice, the guys heard a southern drawl ask, "Mind if I play?" Hawkins Hawk team captain Billy Bob Pruitt eyed the skinny guy's long sideburns and agreed to loan him some shorts and sneakers. Elvis convinced Scotty and Bill (his bass player and drummer) to join in. Legend has it that "team Elvis" scored more than twenty points during the scrimmage. Whatever the truth, that day, the Hawks enjoyed a basketball practice they, most assuredly, would never forget.

That night, the gym was packed—at that time, probably out of curiosity if nothing else. Elvis was still not "Elvis." Most folks in Hawkins did not own a television, but they did turn out, along with hundreds of their curious neighbors from Big Sandy, Gladewater and Pritchett.

After enticing the pumped-up crowd for several excruciating minutes, the star of the show jumped on the stage with legs gyrating and lip snarling. He fired off with "Hearts of Stone" and was drowned out by the roar of the audience. In what was to become almost expected in the years to come, girls of all ages screamed, cried and jumped in their saddle oxfords. In *Elvis in Texas*, Oberst writes that the show ended—literally—with "Shake, Rattle, and Roll."

The kids went home, and the band packed up the Bellaire and headed back to Shreveport for their regular Saturday night gig. That Sunday morning, the senior entrepreneurs were sentenced to sit and submit to the "hellfire and brimstone" hurled down by Deacon Smith from the Baptist pulpit. The kids, no doubt, smiled inwardly. It all, most certainly, was worth every bit. Smith vowed that his town and school would never again submit to the "devil's music" and "sexual inn-u-endos," and he was true to his word. Elvis never performed at the Hawkins gym again.

He sold out his next show at the much larger Hawkins rec center.

CHAPTER 11

MUSIC IN AN OLD GYM

BY BOB BOWMAN

On weekend nights at Lovelady, a small town south of Crockett in Houston County, it's not unusual to hear country music wafting through the rafters of an old school gymnasium.

About eighteen years ago, Norma Dell Jones, the valedictorian of Lovelady High School in 1952, learned that the old gym she knew so well was likely to be torn down.

She rallied others who loved the old gym and put together a restoration effort that led to the gym becoming the center of Lovelady community events and a popular country music venue in east Texas.

Norma Dell, a former schoolteacher at Lovelady, Porter Springs and Crockett, has helped bring to Lovelady, a town of about six hundred people, such country music notables as Noel Lee Haggard, Casey Rivers, Carl Acuff Jr., Hank Thompson, Tommy Horton, Johnny Rodriquez and Branson, Missouri star Moe Bandy, who has played at the gym five times.

"It's a wonderful place to play," said Bandy. "The folks are enthusiastic, and you always leave with a wonderful feeling in your heart."

Bandy was playing on the night we visited the gym. So was Jaye Kelley, a Houston police officer who has appeared with ZZ Top. Kelley belted out Patsy Cline songs as good as Patsy did in her heyday.

Mason Roach, an eight-year-old guitar picker who never had a music lesson, also performed, playing "The House of the Rising Sun."

Top: In an assembly sponsored by the Beaumont High School Student Council, the ever-popular Johnny & The Jammers, led by Johnny Winter, knock out a rock 'n' roll number. Brother Edgar is on the piano. The year is 1968. *Photo provided courtesy of Jim Geuther.*

Bottom: Just before their popularity skyrocketed, "That Lil' ol' Band from Texas" played the prom in the gym at what was then tiny Little-Cypress-Mauriceville. *Photo provided courtesy of the LCM yearbook.*

Visiting the gym on Saturday nights is like going to a friend's home. People in Lovelady are likely to show up with cakes, pies and other food for the visiting bands. The food is also for the show crowds, but at a small cost.

Gene Watson, a country legend with a golden voice, will perform on Friday night, October 16. Watson is a down-to-earth east Texan who was born at Palestine and grew up at Paris.

The Diamond Back Band will appear on Saturday, November 21, and the Quebe Sisters will perform on Saturday, December 12.

Down the calendar will be performances by Tommy Horton with Box Car Bob, Cactus Willie and the Drifters. And Moe Bandy will be back on Saturday, August 20, 2010.

But the gym is also used for weddings, church events, class and family reunions. Davy Crockett's descendants will show up for a reunion next June.

But even with the music performances and family reunions, the Lovelady gym still has the feeling of a gym. The gym's old score clock still hangs on the wall—quietly waiting for a basketball team to show up.

Bob Bowman's East Texas, September 13, 2009. The weekly column is syndicated in 109 east Texas newspapers.
Copyright Bob Bowman

CHAPTER 12

GYMS FROM A BYGONE ERA

AFRICAN AMERICAN SCHOOLS AND THE PVIL

As discussed elsewhere in this book, minority students in Texas historically received very poor treatment. In 1896, the infamous ruling by the U.S. Supreme Court in *Plessy v. Ferguson* found Louisiana's "separate but equal" law constitutional. As a result, African American and Hispanic students in Texas were educated separately from whites. However, it was clear that facilities, equipment, teaching supplies and instruction were anything but equal.

This was just "the way things were" until 1954, when the Supreme Court finally ruled, in *Brown v. Board of Education*, that segregation was illegal (not to mention immoral), and all public schools were ordered to integrate. Unfortunately, the court offered no suggestions as to exactly how this could be done; the transition was anything but smooth. In Texas, by August 1955, several districts announced plans for some form of integration, but meaningful action was not implemented on a large scale until the mid-1960s.

The Prairie View Interscholastic League (PVIL) played a leading role in developing African American students in the arts, literature, athletics and music from the 1920s through 1967. The PVIL served as the governing body for extracurricular activities for Texas's African American high schools.

The structure and format was similar to the University Interscholastic League (UIL); PVIL program administration included athletic and academic competition. At its peak, there were more than 500 African American schools in Texas, including more than 150 high schools.

The beautiful Douglas gym in Cleveland.

The PVIL staged state championship games in football, basketball, baseball and track. Former PVIL Texans include Barbara Jordan, Gene Upshaw, Charley Taylor and Joe Greene.

During the summer of 1965, the UIL State Executive Committee validated the Legislative Council's decision to open league membership to all public schools, so the PVIL began to merge with the UIL at the start of the 1967–68 school year. The league was officially disbanded at the end of the 1969–70 school year.

While it may seem incredible today, high school athletics in Texas were also kept "separate but equal." "Colored" gymnasiums were often ramshackle wooden structures without indoor plumbing or adequate heat. There are few of these old buildings still standing today, much less still in use by local school districts.

Fortunately, there are a few of these beautiful gyms still around. But "back in the day," the run-down gyms in various stages of disrepair could do nothing to put a damper on the excitement and joy of the great matches that regularly took place in these old barns.

Today, it's interesting to consider that, surely, some of the greatest high school games ever played took place in these buildings. Likewise, leading these games were some of the greatest, most legendary coaches of all time.

The ceiling of the Douglas gym highlights the wonderful handiwork of WPA workers.

Above: The Fred Moore gym in Denton is well maintained and still used today.

Right: Inside the Fred Moore gym.

One such example of a great coach who, while very successful, emphasized the importance of raising good citizens was Lural McCloud. When he passed away on July 18, 2008, Coach McCloud left behind scores of young men who may have learned basketball, but they also learned much, much more.

After he was discharged from the army in the early 1950s, McCloud took the basketball coaching job at Madisonville Marian Anderson High School, an all-black school that competed in the PVIL. Starting out, the program had nothing. He had to "beg, borrow, and steal" just to have uniforms for his players. Often, Coach McCloud gave his boys money out of his own pocket so he knew they would not go into a game hungry.

Lural McCloud, coach, role model and friend to hundreds of students in Cleveland.

"We won state championships," said McCloud, "but the main thing we tried to do was motivate youngsters to become good citizens, good people."

Regarded by those who knew him as a gentle giant, McCloud stayed on as head basketball coach at Madisonville High School after integration, but his philosophy of dedication and hard work remained unchanged.

Former Madisonville athletic director Jerry Harper remembered Coach McCloud as a very positive person with "a wonderful personality, good-natured, just a great fellow." Harper said, "The kids loved him, and the adults loved his sense of humor." Harper's son-in-law, Billy Rigby, was first coached by McCloud, then later coached with him.

"My son-in-law thought he hung the moon," said Harper.

Long before the days of "no pass, no play," McCloud would routinely check on his players' grades and make sure they were doing well with their coursework. If a player was not passing, he would not play. It was not unusual for a player to miss practice to go to tutorials for extra help.

A few months before he died, Coach Mac, as McCloud's players called him, attended a reunion at the Marian Anderson School, and many former students credited him with contributing to what they are today. Man after man spoke of how important Coach Mac was in their lives, yet the coach had no idea that he had influenced so many young people in such a positive way.

Lural McCloud was a true humanitarian. He was a teacher, a husband, a father, a minister and a friend…and Coach.

CHAPTER 13

A SAD FATE FOR THE MOST BEAUTIFUL GYM IN TEXAS

The old gym at Antelope, Texas, is one of the most beautiful examples of WPA craftmanship anywhere. Long since abandoned (the school closed in 1972), this stone masterpiece is still a wonderful gym to see.

Today, Antelope is not much of a place at all. It's about twenty miles northwest of Jacksboro in northwestern Jack County. The settlement itself is quite old. Records indicate that B.F. Spears was appointed the town's first postmaster in 1859, and by 1890, the town had a population of three hundred, complete with a hotel, several churches, general stores and a school. Probably the biggest boost to the area was the stage from Henrietta and Graham that passed through Antelope daily. In 1900, the gristmill was replaced by a cotton gin as the town's biggest business.

Unfortunately, after the stage service was discontinued, the numbers began to dwindle. By 1914, the population was two hundred, and the gin and the hotels were gone. Finally, by the late 1900s, the population had fallen to around sixty, and only two businesses remained.

However, there remains one of the most magnificent gyms in Texas. Each time I visit, it's more run-down. The WPA plaque remains right by the front door. The scoreboard and backboards are still in place, too, but that's about it. The wooden floor is warped and buckled and rotted. Though supported by sturdy trusses, the roof is slowly allowing the elements to come through. But, without a doubt, when anyone steps in, the visitor is transported back in time.

Inside the Antelope gym. *Photo by Bret Cococcia.*

In addition to the native stone structure, the construction project for the gym included a septic tank, a disposal field and improved school facilities, and it employed approximately twenty laborers. Of the total cost of $21,393, $13,622 was provided by the WPA, while the local school district provided the remainder.

IN THE *TIMES RECORD NEWS* of January 28, 2008, Lara K. Richards wrote a story featuring the old Antelope Gym.

> The "Home of the Antlers" is now home to nothing but faded glory. The once shining gymnasium, a Works Progress Administration project, is boarded up and vacant.
>
> Edward "Shine" Leach, a 1948 Antelope High School graduate, remembers when the new facility was completed in 1940.
>
> "When they built that building, nobody could get out there on the court without their good shoes on. That was a big no-no," he said. "That thing shined. It was the most blessed thing we'd had in our community in a while."
>
> Before the new gym was completed, kids played ball on a dirt court in back of the school.
>
> "We'd been playing out on the dirt with all the wind blowing and everything," he said. "It was a blessing, the new gym."
>
> Don Guice joined the Antelope school system in 1943 as a ninth-grader. "At the time, the gym was probably one of the best ones in the 1940s in this part of the country, because most of the gyms back then, you played on a stage in the auditorium where the basketball court was," he said.
>
> The main attraction in the building was the large gymnasium with its high ceiling. Four rows of built-in wooden bleachers lined both walls, crowding the court.
>
> Dan Webb, seventy-two, who went to school in Midway in Clay County, remembers playing in the building. "One of the most vivid memories I have is of the supports on each side," he said about the beams running from floor-to-ceiling a foot or so from the court. "You had to be very careful when you were playing that you didn't crash into them."
>
> And then there were the goals, positioned just a few inches from the edge of the court, he said. "The out-of-bounds line was right there on the wall," he said. "You didn't want to go up too fast on a lay-up or you'd be plastered on the wall."
>
> Guice said the local boys called it the "out-of-bounds wall," he joked about the concrete brick wall. "It was pretty close. Used to, a lot of the gyms would have pads on the wall, but we never had them," he laughed.

IMPORTANT (SAD) NOTICE

This note was posted December 30, 2016, on the "Living New Deal" website.

> *I regret to inform you that the antelope gym has been torn down due to dilapidation and danger to community. There are rocks on the site available for salvage. My husband played many games in that gym, and roller skated too. My in-laws enjoyed the gym when it was first built. It was beautiful. So sad.*

I felt obligated to travel, one last time, to see the status of the Antelope gym for myself.

Such is the fate of so many of our old gyms. In many ways, it's inevitable.

*Author's note: I visited this gym three times. This story was written in 2008.

The Antelope gym today.

CHAPTER 14

SAMNORWOOD

WHERE SCHOOL WAS A FAMILY AFFAIR

S mall-town schools have things in common. For example, most small, rural districts must count every penny; budgets are always tight. More noticeably, the school is quite likely the largest employer in town. School history and family history are often intertwined. Generations attend the same school, often taught by the same teachers. Many of us have heard "You're nothing like your brother" from veteran teachers. In my case, I don't think it was intended as a compliment.

Samnorwood was named for early county leader Samuel Norwood, but Samnorwood was hardly the only town in Texas named for one of its founders. It joined the ranks of places like Tomball, Tom Bean and Edcouch. Sam was an English rancher who was drawn to the area because of the enormous availability of land.

A true original rugged pioneer, Norwood remained a leader in the community until he died, in Samnorwood, at the age of ninety-eight.

Located in northern Collingsworth County in the southeast panhandle, Samnorwood still scratches out a hard living by farming and ranching. The village really sprang to life in the early 1930s, when the Fort Worth and Denver Northern Railway established a route from Childress to Pampa, which ran right through Samnorwood.

The grand opening was quite the affair. It was July 4, 1931, and the townspeople gathered not only for the Independence Day picnic, but also for the opening of the depot. A barbershop, a café, a cotton gin and two general stores soon prospered. The post office opened in October 1932, and after

Samnorwood gym today.

that, the beautiful brick high school—complete with gymnasium—opened its doors for students in the fall of 1934 at a cost of $25,000. The Samnorwood School also educated children from neighboring Abra, Aberdeen, Round-up and several others.

The Oldham family of Samnorwood, Texas, was involved in the school almost from the beginning and was certainly there until the end. Pretty Helen Lang was one of the first students enrolled when the school doors were thrown open in 1934. She was also a cheerleader on the first squad for the Samnorwood Cats in 1937. Later, she married Samnorwood boy Albert Oldham, and they raised their family there.

In what probably almost seemed inevitable at that time, the population in the area dwindled, as did local enterprise and student enrollment. By 1984, Samnorwood pretty much had only the school, the post office, one store and a church. By the turn of the century, the population had dwindled to thirty-nine. The secondary grades were discontinued in 2011, and the school closed its doors for good—to all students—the very next year, as students were transported to Wellington.

But the Oldham family is still there. When a school is closed, every community is faced with the dilemma of what to do with the old building. In Samnorwood, when the school closed, local boy Gary Oldham just bought the darn thing. And why not? He is Albert and Helen's son, so he's lived in the same house in Samnorwood for sixty-two years. He married a girl from Shamrock, and she taught in Samnorwood for twenty years. Gary's

Like in almost all old gyms, the trophy case is in the gym lobby. Remembrances of past victories.

dad served on the school board for ten years, and Gary served for twenty-five years, until 2003, when their last child graduated.

The Oldhams' daughter, Cheyenne, once won the bronze medal in the state meet in Austin in the 200-meter dash. The Eagles did have a basketball team go to state, but it did not win. However, the school had several state and national championships in Future Farmers of America (FFA) and UIL academic and musical events over the years.

At over six hundred square miles, Samnorwood was one of the largest districts in the state. It was once a consolidation of seventeen schools in the area. At its peak, the school boasted an enrollment of more than five hundred students.

Since he bought the school, Gary now run his family business, SOS From Texas Organic Cotton Products, from the old school library. However, he never seems to be too busy to let a "tourist" look around, and he might even open the gym and turn on the lights. It's a beautiful old gym.

THERE IS NOTHING SADDER than an empty school. Schools are built for children, and when the noise, excitement and energy are gone, the old building feels especially silent. Empty gyms are cavernous vaults of sadness. The laughs, the squeals and squeaks and dribbles and thuds are no longer there; only in our memories can we recall these warm memories.

CHAPTER 15

GYM RUINS

When meandering around central Texas, travelers on FM 1864 are often surprised to see what could be a Roman ruin. Instead, it's the remains of the old gymnasium from the Scranton School.

Early settlers to the area were two pairs of brothers, D.C. and H.B. Lane and Joe and Aaron Brown, who, by 1880, had a gin and a school. By the turn of the century, they had a post office and the Scranton Academy. The academy was quite a progressive concept at the time. It was a coeducational preparatory school with a curriculum that offered a science program (complete with a modern lab), a library and a teacher training program. It had separate dormitories for girls and boys, a five-hundred-seat auditorium and several athletic fields. At its peak, the Scranton Academy boasted an enrollment of more than 350 students.

During this time, the town also flourished. Until World War I, the town had added a dry goods store, a hardware store, two grocery stores and a newspaper.

Sadly, the war devastated the Scranton Academy, as most of the older boys withdrew from school to enlist. As a result, the school closed in 1914.

In addition, in 1917, a boll weevil epidemic destroyed the cotton industry in the area, so most farmers were forced to switch to peanuts for their cash crop.

The Great Depression continued to bring hardship to Scranton, as most able-bodied men left for Fort Worth looking for work. One good thing that did happen during the 1930s was that the WPA came to Scranton to build

Standing inside the old Scranton gym.

Outside the southern wall.

the magnificent gym. This stone building was part of the community even after the school closed in 1964. Sadly, the economy did not rebound after World War II, and the public school closed in 1964. A fire in 1968 gutted the empty school, and a few walls of the old gym are all that's left.

Today, there's only a handful of people left; there are no businesses and no post office.

At the site stands a marker honoring Coach Clinton "Shorty" Adams and members of the Scranton Academy basketball team for 1915–16. The team was made up of thirteen players with names like Graydon, Otis, Potsy and Babe.

That year, the boys were a cool 28–0, and that's not too shabby!

CHAPTER 16

DARROUZETT

THE TOWN YOU CAN'T GET TO FROM HERE

Way back in 1917, the tiny, far north panhandle town of Darrouzett sprang to life because the Santa Fe railroad ran a track near where the Plummer and Kiowa Creeks met. The town was originally called "Lourwood," after Opal Lourwood, the first child born there. However, the apple-polishing forefathers readily changed the name to Darrouzett, for State Representative (as well as railroad official) John Lewis Darrouzet.

In just a couple of years, Darrouzett was incorporated and boasted various businesses, two churches, a school, a post office and 425 people.

Nowadays, the three hundred or so folks who live in Darrouzett, Texas, have heard all the jokes. In fact, the citizens themselves are quite proud and boast that their town is "the best paved town per capita of the Panhandle." The more poetic souls like to note that Darrouzett is "an island in a sea of grass."

While that all may or may not be so, Darrouzett is the home of the Longhorns and home to one of the coolest gyms in Texas.

Lifelong resident Ernie Miller fondly remembers his days as a basketball player for the Longhorns.

"The locker rooms are under the bleachers, so when we were getting dressed for our game, the girls were playing," recalls Miller.

The girls' game was different then. In Texas, until 1978, the girls played a half-court game. Teams of six—three forwards and three guards—would compete. Only forwards were permitted to shoot the ball, and the guards only played defense. Of course, there was no three-point line.

Above: Darrouzett gym, home of the Longhorns.

Left: Inside the Darrouzett gym.

But the games were no less exciting. Miller remembers the fans stomping and cheering. Many brought in noise-making devices, and the home crowd could get very loud, especially when its archrivals, the Follett Panthers, came to town.

While the exterior of the gym sports clean, distinctive lines, it's the interior that makes this gym unique. For one thing, the gym is still used every day. It's the only gym the kids from Darrouzett have ever known.

View
from the
baseline.

From their earliest days as Little Dribblers, to their final game as seniors, the Longhorn gym was home.

However, the most noticeable thing is that the interior looks like it could be a gigantic hunting lodge. The entire interior—the bleachers, the walls and even the locker rooms—are constructed with beautiful knotty pine.

Ernie Miller believes the gym was made of knotty pine simply because that was the material available at the time. If that's indeed the case, generations of Darrouzett kids of have benefited from one of the most magnificent—and unique—gyms in the state. Better yet, the gym will no doubt continue to be the home of future Longhorns for generations to come.

In case you're interested, here are "some lies about Darrouzett":

> • *a huge wolverine was seen at North Fork Kiowa Creek after midnight heaving rocks into the flow*
> • *a giant javelina can be seen on top of Indian Hill at night staring off into the distance*
> • *a space alien became visible in the backseat of a car by the driver catching a glimpse of the ghost in her rearview mirror at night.*

CHAPTER 17

THE GHOSTS IN THE OLD DUBLIN GYM

BY PATTY HIRST

I t's not only the people, but also some places around town that make Dublin, Texas, so special. Mention "the old gym" and allow just a moment…it's like opening a faucet full blast!

Built by the Work Projects Administration (WPA) during the Depression, *the old gym* is an *institution* for multiple generations of Dubliners.

Since 1940, can you imagine how many people have sat in the stands, played on the court, attended or participated in events in what has been a gathering place for the community for more than seventy years?

Until the fall of 1986, every student attending Dublin ISD was in one of the buildings on North Camden Street. The gym was at the heart of that *complex* and every student in pre-K through the twelfth grade had a turn in that wonderful old rock structure for one reason or another.

Even though I have attended events of all kinds there since 1981, Friday afternoon pep rallies are synonymous with that special spot in my mind.

I had participated in pep rallies during my own junior high and high school days and attended countless ones throughout college and prior teaching assignments, but until I attended my first Dublin Lions pep rally in the fall of 1981, my point of reference was lacking.

Each week during football season, the stands were packed! They were so full that the youngest elementary kids were ringed around the court in rows and seated on the floor so that everyone could attend; the student body functioned as just that—one united force—one body!

Much to the chagrin of the folks in Shamrock, Dublin claims to be the "Irish Capital of Texas." The old gym at Dublin still looks great today.

The air was electric. When the football players came in that back door, the crowd literally leapt to its feet and clapped in rhythm as the band blasted "Rocky" from the south bleachers.

If *school spirit* was in the dictionary, a picture of one of those pep rallies would be the definition! Wow! I got carried away there myself, and that was just a fraction of one of those Friday afternoon experiences.

By the fall of 1986, the *new elementary* behind the football field on Thomas Street had become home to pre-K through fifth grades, and not having the whole district present each week relieved some of the overcrowding, but it was a little like having some of the family missing.

So many other incredible occasions have taken place within those noble rock walls.

In talking to former students, they came up with a long list of *times remembered*. How hot it was, the big fans that were so loud, running bleachers at basketball practice, the smell in the dressing rooms came to mind.

The trophy case in the foyer, the concession stand that served as the snack bar during school lunch time, donkey basketball games played for fundraisers, Project Graduation...

When Dublin held its chamber banquet there, it was really hard for me to concentrate on the program; I kept thinking of the hours I had spent there, the people, the great memories...

CHAPTER 18

TWO MAGNIFICENT GYMS STILL IN USE TODAY

Personal favorites of mine are when I find beautiful old gyms that are still in use—and still needed—today. Here are two such gyms.

Moran ISD is in Shackelford County in north central Texas, and Morgan Mill ISD is about eighty-five miles to the east in central Erath County.

Both are magnificent examples of the artistry of the skilled laborers employed by the WPA, and seeing these gyms today is like stepping back in time some seventy-five years.

MORAN

The town of Moran came about when the Texas Central Railroad came through in 1882. After a couple of tries, the residents named their village "Moran" to honor the railroad president, John J. Moran.

Like most of the small towns in that area of Texas, Moran reached its economic peak in the early 1940s because of the thriving oil and gas industry, when the town boasted a population of some 710 citizens. Like the rest of the area, the population dwindled as the industry waned. By 1950, it had declined to 610; by 1980, there were 344 people calling Moran home. At this time, there were still two grain elevators, three churches and the school.

The public school was created after the election of April 4, 1908, decreed that the town of Moran would "incorporate for free school purposes only" for its first public school.

Above: The beautiful Moran gym and wall. Built by the WPA.

Left: The wall was constructed out of surplus rock by the WPA.

The Moran gym interior.

View from the bleachers.

Due to student growth, the school expanded with a new, larger high school, complete with all of the "modern conveniences" in 1923. About that same time, the Moran student body selected the sobriquet "Bulldogs," as it is to this day.

In 1938 and 1939, WPA tradesmen constructed the Moran High School gymnasium. In 1940, WPA workers constructed the now-familiar rock fence around the campus. The gymnasium, with its wooden basketball court and stone walls, is still in use today and is the oldest building on the MHS campus.

MORGAN MILL

The history of the first Morgan Mill School begins on March 21, 1879, when two acres of land were deeded to the community for school purposes.

In 1906, a new two-story schoolhouse was constructed on what is now the present site of the Morgan Mill School land. In 1918, that school was destroyed by fire. A four-room, limestone rock school building was then erected on the same site. The schoolchildren attended classes in the churches while the schoolhouse was being built.

In 1939, the WPA started construction on the new school. The first classes were held in the new building in September 1940, as some of the classrooms had been completed by that time. The gymnasium, the rock wall perimeter and other structures were completed in 1941.

The gym is one of the few remaining WPA school buildings still in use in Erath County. It has been the hub of many community activities for more than seven decades, and that's not likely to change in the foreseeable future.

In the summer of 2006, I had an appointment with the superintendent of tiny Morgan Mill ISD to see its old gym. As is usually the case, when you visit a school in the summer, some serious work is going on. Summer is the time to paint, shampoo the carpets, strip and wax the floors and run through the regular "to do" lists for school maintenance.

In that regard, small school districts are a little different. Arriving at Morgan Mill High School, I met a custodian who was stripping and waxing the floor in the main hallway. I asked him where I might find the superintendent. He laughed and said, "You found him!"

The custodian/principal/superintendent was Dean Edwards. In 2016, Edwards retired after serving as superintendent there for thirty-one years.

View from the baseline in the beautiful Morgan Mill gym.

The bleachers are along just one side of the gym.

Morgan Mill boasts a "big-assed fan." It really helps move the air in the small gym.

This view from the "cheap seats" proves that there is no bad seat in the Morgan Mill gym.

According to Edwards, Morgan Mill is a special place. For example, "If a fella is riding down the road on his tractor, and he sees the football field needs mowing, he'll just turn in and take care of it." One year, the teachers decided they would rather share a very small stipend to clean their own classrooms, rather than hire a custodian. A few years before, after a rash of injuries to the six-man football team, the already undermanned Mustangs were going to have to cancel the rest of their season and forfeit the rest of their games. That was until Dean got to work early Monday morning and met three girls—including his own daughter—on the front steps of the school. The girls told him, "We're cheerleaders, but without a team we won't have anything to cheer about!" So, for the first time in those parts, girls played varsity football, and the season was saved. The team more than held its own, winning more games than it lost.

However, the most noteworthy thing about the Morgan Mill school is the old gym. Made with local stones, the gym is quaint and extremely cool. Bleachers run along one side of the gym, and the floor itself sports a three-point line that runs right out of bounds. Ivy adorns the outer walls and even sneaks inside a gym window and down the interior wall.

Another beautiful thing about this gym is that it's the only gym in the school district. The facility is used all day, every day, by kids of all ages. Most folks who live in Morgan Mill played in that gym. Since the student enrollment has changed very little over the last forty years, it seems likely that the old gym will remain in use for the foreseeable future.

That's a really good thing.

CHAPTER 19

ACTIVITIES WE LOVED IN THE OLD GYM

The old gyms that stir our memories are not only remembered for athletic events. The gym was the place for dances, pep rallies, fundraisers, graduations, band concerts, beauty pageants and so much more.

Alumni from the old Reagan Gym remember roller skating, donkey basketball, class plays and Halloween carnivals.

Can you imagine what today's basketball coaches might say if someone approached them and asked, "Hey, coach. How about tonight, after the game, we let all the kids roller-skate on the gym floor?"

Right.

The tiny town of Reagan is about forty miles southeast of Waco. The small school was closed in 1948, and students were sent to Marlin, but the alumni organization is still very active today.

On his website forttumbleweed.net, former Reagan Bearkat Len Kubiak writes:

> *West of the school cafeteria building stood the stately gymnasium building which would have rivaled a lot of colleges in its time. This building was well known by all members of the community. It was here that pageants were put on at Easter, Christmas and Thanksgiving and it was here that Marilyn Scroggins once performed a beautiful piano recital.*
>
> *The Reagan Gym was a marvel of a building that served the needs of the school, town and area communities. At the back of the gym was a large*

There's nothing quite like a junior high dance.

A dance at the old gym at Kennedale in 1971.

stage that was used for class plays, square dancing, musical performances, and travelling country/western shows including the Hank Williams show. To either side of the gym were the boys and girls dressing rooms.

As a young lad, I can still remember the antique football helmets and equipment that had been used by Reagan athletes since the turn of the century. Although the gym was primarily built for musical performances and basketball, the Reagan gym also doubled as a skating rink, a Halloween Carnival with room enough for the entire population of Reagan to attend, a dance hall, site for the prom, graduation ceremonies, and a roller skating rink. The gym was also used as a recreation center for the churches, 4-H clubs, Home Demonstration Clubs, square dancing, traveling movie shows, music recitals and country and western shows.

One of the special shows was put on by the Sinclair Oil Corporation during which a multitude of oil products were given away as door prizes. I remember winning a can of oil. (Now, what was a ten-year-old kid in Reagan gonna do with a can of oil? Why, oil the chains of all the kids' bicycles, of course). It's too bad the old school gym had to be torn down. It was our skating rink, basketball court and concert hall all rolled into one. Does anyone recall the donkey basketball game we had one time? Did anyone score a goal?

CHAPTER 20

CONCLUSION

REMEMBER THE OLD GYM?

I n the small, sleepy town of Anywhere, Texas, there is an old, worn-out high school gym. No doubt, you've passed by it many times and wondered about its history.

Was it an old WPA project built by our anxious, Depression-era grandparents or great-grandparents, frantic to feed their families while keeping a worried glance toward Europe and the dark storm brewing there?

Today, members of the community, who are often the grandchildren of the creators of the wonderful building, are contemplating the fate of the old gym.

Maybe the plan is to re-purpose the 1937 building into a senior citizens' center, or as a place to be used by the youth and all citizens of the community for cultural events and creative art shows, dances or reunions.

We applaud these noble intentions, but these gyms are more special to us than just for the memories we hold so dear. They are cherished because of more than the games played or dances attended. There's something more real, more tangible.

There is a wonderful—and crucial—part of our younger days that we don't talk about much, and maybe we should: the sweet, spicy, sharp, stinging scent of the old gymnasiums. These old gyms, with their slightly sagging stages, were where the one-act plays, Christmas band concerts, beauty pageants and talent shows were held.

Remember the side baskets that folded up to the ceiling when needed? And why did they all have to be manually cranked with a very shaky fifty-foot pole that could only be properly accomplished by the gruff wizard of a janitor who knew where everything was and could fix anything? Not to mention, he would clean up all accidents—no matter how gross—without complaint. Heck, in a pinch, he could splint broken fingers and locate ice for swollen ankles.

There were also some home-court advantages. Only the home team knew where those dead spots were on that creaking, golden and dusty wooden floor. In addition, only the home team knew that the basket on one end was one inch higher than the hoop at the other end!

In some gyms, the bleachers were folded—shrieking and groaning—back up against the wall to leave more room to work out. This took a tremendous feat of strength from the whole team, and even from the coach or any dads who may have been loitering about, waiting to watch practice. It also required feats of strength to open (and close) the immense, ancient windows, which also had to be cranked open with yet another long, rusty metal pole.

Of course, the old gyms had the archaic locker rooms under the bleachers with rusted showers no one dared use, for fear of lockjaw. These dungeons were most likely imported whole and untouched from the catacombs of ancient Rome.

Finally, there was a large metal basket in the supply closet used to store the flaccid basketballs, rubbery dodgeballs and stained, moldy softballs and baseballs.

Occasionally, an unfortunate sparrow would be frantically captured in the gym because the kids would prop open the emergency exit doors to, hopefully, get at least a breath of air in the place.

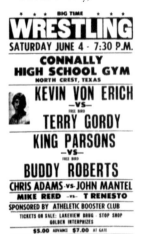

Pro wrestling came to the gym for fundraising.

Lost and forgotten behind the massive stage curtains was quite an eclectic collection of stray, crusty gym socks, waterlogged mathematics textbooks, obsolete volumes of *Encyclopaedia Britannica* and assorted hall passes. Not to mention it's where one would find most of the props from Christmas pageants past, supplies for the Valentine's Day dance and unopened boxes of copier paper.

Finally, there are the old baskets' battered backboards themselves. Once white, but now a sort of pearl gray, complete with ghostly imprints of thousands of bad shots stamped faintly on

Students perform the maypole dance for their parents in the Samnorwood gym in the 1950s.

the wood, there are still remnants of the silvery nylon game nets. Oddly, even the new nets never seemed whole for more than a game or so, but the coaches (or, more likely, the old janitor) would stitch them back together for each home game.

Of course, can we forget the two referees? They could have been sent to us straight from central casting. Aging and slightly paunchy now, one tall, the other short, and one sporting a hard-fought comb-over, you had better believe they were absolute in their authority and quick to issue technical fouls for what they construed as disrespect of the game.

Remember the squeak and squeal of sneakers during basketball, volleyball, dodgeball or kickball games, accompanied by the squeaks and squeals of the kids wearing them? It was here the thought occurs to me that maybe this was the sweetest sound of all. It was so open and innocent and untrammeled, created by sheer, wild, headlong, passionate joy. The music was all those sneakers, and the kids who wore them, and the gym, the cathedral in which they played.

Remember?

THE OLD GYM AT Waelder has surely seen better days, but the wildcatted mural remains on guard, forever vigilant. If a Round Top Cub or Dime Box Longhorn ventures his way, even now, he'll be waiting.

Some of the old gyms are forced to endure the indignity of sharing a communal parking lot with the new gym; the juxtaposition is startling. Our gym, once state of the art, is now an afterthought, a problem for the community. Once the home of varsity championships, playoff games and proms, it's now relegated to the Saturday morning Little Dribblers and peewee cheer camps. If your travels ever take you by Perico, McAdoo or Duffau, why don't you stop by the old gym for a few minutes? Walk around, take in the smells and listen for the echoes. Before you know it, a couple of hours will just disappear. It's a lovely way to spend an afternoon.

The Waelder Wildcat remains on guard on the old gym wall. Today, the gym is mostly used for storage.

LAYUPS

I n basketball, layups are often the quickest—and easiest—way to score. Hence, the last part of *Historic Texas Gyms: A Tribute to Vanishing Traditions* is a brief scatter shooting of photos from interesting gyms from all over the state. Unless noted otherwise, all images are provided courtesy of the author. Enjoy!

Playground equipment behind the old gym at Millersview appears to be ready for the recess bell to ring. *Photo provided courtesy of Randy James.*

A few miles from Millersview is an almost identical gym in Eola. During the Great Depression, it was not unusual for schools to reuse plans from other projects. The gym in Eola is now a brewery.

The main entrance to the magnificent Navasota gym, home of the Rattlers.

The stage still adorns the magnificent gym in Toyah. *Photo provided courtesy of Randy James.*

Standing on the baseline in the beautiful stone gym in Claude, home of the Mustangs and Lady 'Stangs. *Photo provided courtesy of Randy James.*

Inside the fabulous WPA rock gym in Duffau, one of my favorite gyms in the state.

Another look inside the great old gym in Gordon. *Photo provided courtesy of Randy James.*

Inside what's left of the old gym at Indian Creek. The beautiful workmanship of the brickmasons is still apparent.

An exterior shot of the McAdoo gym.

Inside the beautiful wooden gym in Tehuacana. Built in the late 1920s, this is another of my favorite gyms. *Photo provided courtesy of Randy James.*

Standing in the parking lot of the cool, old WPA rock gym in Slidell, home of the Greyhounds.

114

A view from the cheap seats inside the old Ponder gym. Fans saw a lot of great basketball in this place.

There is not a prettier example of WPA workmanship than the splendid rock gym in Winnsboro.

Left: Inside the mess that is the old gym at Noodle/Crossroads. *Photo provided courtesy of John Grigsby.*

Below: Outside view of the gym at Noodle/Crossroads. *Photo provided courtesy of John Grigsby.*

This magnificent gym in Luling is one of the finest examples of WPA workmanship anywhere.

The incredible old WPA gym and rock wall at Navasota.

Left: The football locker room was in the old gym at Navasota. On Friday nights, the Rattlers descended one hundred steps to the field below.

Below: Just about all that's left of the tiny Hardeman County town of Goodlett is this pristine WPA-era gymnasium. It remains a pleasant surprise to travelers heading west on U.S. Highway 287. Just eight miles out of Quanah, today the gym serves as a church.

Inside the Brackettville gym.

The massive old gym at Childress was built in 1929.

The gym at Evant is another wonderfully maintained WPA project.

Inside the Evant gym.

Above: The West Columbia gym, home of the Roughnecks and Lady Necks.

Right: The view from the home bleachers in the West Columbia gym.

The gym at Rockdale is beautifully maintained.

Beautiful workmanship accents the
Rockdale gym.

Above: Standing on the baseline of the still gorgeous Adams gym, it's easy to see why folks in Lockhart are rightfully proud of their old gym.

Right: Inside the old barn at Crossroads, there is very little evidence this ever was a gym.

But, if you look hard enough, there is proof that kids played here.

The gym at Little River Academy is home of the Bumblebees, as well as many championships.

The home bleachers in the Cumby gym.

Above: The magnificent ruins of Mosheim School. *Below*: Hallway inside the school. *Photos provided courtesy of Randy James.*

The gym at Shamrock. *Photo provided courtesy of Randy James.*

The WPA gym at Hamilton.

Left: The soil around the old gym at Pyote seems excellent for cactus.

Middle: However, the ruin of the old gym has seen better days. *Photo provided courtesy of John Grigsby*.

Bottom: The old gym at Oklahoma Lane is now a beautiful church.

Inside the church at Oklahoma Lane.

The beautiful old rock gym at Wortham was built in 1940. *Photo provided courtesy of Randy James.*

Top: The beautiful WPA rock gym and wall at Whitehouse.

Bottom: The wonderful rock gym at Harmony, home of the Eagles.

Left: The gym at Goodrich, home of the Hornets. *Photo courtesy of John Grigsby*. *Right*: The Junction Eagle still stands guard, ready to intimidate any visitor to the Eagle gym. The construction of the Junction gym was truly a community effort.

The magnificent ghostly structure of the old gym at McAdoo. *Photo provided courtesy of Randy James*.

Above: The concession counter inside the McAdoo gym.

Left: Exit beside the bleachers inside the McAdoo gym.

Opposite, top: Standing at half-court in the old McAdoo gym.

Opposite, bottom: The view from the baseline. *Photo provided courtesy of Randy James.*

This was once a shower in the old gym at McAdoo.

Left: Way out in Big Bend country, tiny Valentine (town population, 135) regularly fields one "boys" team made up of the entire student body. In 2014, that consisted of 4 boys and 3 girls. In Valentine, the old gym truly is the main meeting place in the community.

Below: The massive old auditorium/gym at Whitewright is magnificent.

Left: The Spring Creek gym, home of the Crawdads.

Below: The old gym at Hondo is now the shop.

The old gym at Lohn is still used every day.

Schulenburg Turner Hall. Built in 1886, this is, likely, the oldest gymnasium in Texas.

Left: The old gym at Wingate has certainly seen better days.

Below: The WPA gym at Taylor is now the Family Resource Center.

Above: The pretty brick gym at San Saba is now the weight room.

Below: View from the bleachers in the old Ranger gym.

The old gym at Dale.

The Ganado gym.

The Gruver gym, home of the Greyhounds. A great feature of the old Gruver gym is a floor that is totally retractable, with a pool underneath, just like the gym floor in the classic film *It's a Wonderful Life. Photo provided courtesy of Randy James.*

Inside the gym at Knox City.

The hallway and trophy case leading into the gym at Pringle.

The old gym at Pringle has been deserted for many years. A few years ago, a fire devastated all that was left. Steel beams literally melted. *Photo provided courtesy of Randy James.*

The old Kennedale gym when it was new, in 1964. *Sketch provided courtesy Kennedale Yearbook.*

A unique aspect of the gym in Bonham is that the entryway for the auditorium is in the front...

...whereas, the gymnasium entrance is in the back.

BIBLIOGRAPHY

Introduction: A Word about the WPA

Records of the Work Projects Administration [WPA]. National Archives and Records Administration. www.archives.gov/research/guide-fed-records/groups/069.html.

"Works Progress Administration (WPA)." A&E Television Networks. July 13, 2017. www.history.com/topics/great-depression/works-progress-administration.

"The Works Progress Administration." Public Broadcasting Service. 2018. www.pbs.org/wgbh/americanexperience/features/surviving-the-dust-bowl-works-progress-administration-wpa.

"Works Progress Administration." *Works Progress Administration*. N.p., n.d. Accessed September 9, 2016. http://www.indiana.edu/~liblilly/wpa/wpa_info.html.

Works Progress Administration Records, 1933–1943. Dolph Briscoe Center for American History, University of Texas at Austin.

Chapter 1: Perico: A Forgotten Gym

Anderson, H. Allen. "Perico, TX." Texas State Historical Association. June 15, 2010. Accessed August 14, 2016.

"Dalhart, Texas Ghost Pictures." Dalhart, Texas, Ghost Pictures. Ghostsofamerica.com. Accessed September 9, 2016. http://www.ghostsofamerica.com/7/Texas_Dalhart_ghost_sightings.

Troesser, John. "Perico, Texas, Texas Panhandle Ghost Town." "The Town We Are Approaching Was Perico." *Texas Escapes* (online magazine). Accessed August 14, 2016. August 3, 2007.

Chapter 2: What If?: Remembering the Tragedy of McCaulley

Guinn, Jeff. "Requiem for a Team." *Star-Telegram*, February 13, 2005. Accessed August 17, 2016. http://www.star.telegram.com.

Kaye, R.A. "Motor Carrier Accident Investigation. Cardinal Surveys Company and McCaulley Independent School District. Accident." December 8, 1978, Roby, Texas, Transport Research International Documentation, TRID. USDOT, April 30, 1984. Accessed August 18, 2016. https://trid.trb.org/view.aspx?id=198542.

"McCaulley, TX." Texas State Historical Association. Texas State Historical Association. June 15, 2010. Accessed August 17, 2016.

Chapter 3: Mr. and Mrs. Fort Stockton

Espino, Billy. Interview with author. June 9, 2006.

"Fort Stockton, Texas." *Fort Stockton Texas; Historic Fort Stockton.* N.p., n.d. Accessed August 24, 2016. http://texasescapes.com/WestTexasTowns/FtStocktonTx/FortStocktonTexas.htm.

Chapter 4: Tragedy Comes to Two Texas Gyms

"Buffalo, TX Aircraft Explosion Kills 34, Sep 1959." *GenDisasters.com.* N.p., n.d. Web. 25 Sept. 2016. http://www3.gendisasters.com/texas/3979/buffalo%2C-tx-aircraft-explosion-kills-34%2C-sep-1959.

"Dawson, Texas Ghost Sightings." *Dawson, Texas, Ghost Sightings.* Ghostsofamerica.com. Accessed September 24, 2016. http://www.ghostsofamerica.com/7/Texas_Dawson_ghost_sightings.html.

Goodwyn, Vanessa. "A Black Day in Buffalo's History: Braniff Crash Revisited." *Leon County Today*, September 9, 2009. Accessed September 24, 2016. http://www.leoncountytoday.com/news/2009-09.

Jacobs, Janet. "Dawson Plane Crash Remembered." *Corsicana Daily Sun*, May 3, 2008. Accessed September 24, 2016. http://www.corsicanadailysun.

com/archives/dawson-plane-crash-remembered/article_54e13070-635d-597c-9fd5-87f475890506.html.

Chapter 5: Aunt Cora Finds a Home

Camenisch, Franna. "Aunt Cora Clinger." *The Deaf Texan* 96, no. 2 (Spring 2011): 13–14. *Texas School for the Deaf Museum and Archives*. Web. 2 Sept. 2016. *San Antonio Express* 48, no. 125, Monday, May 5, 1913.

Hassell, Jerry, "Profile of a Successful Alumna: Aunt Cora Clinger," *Lone Star* (Spring 2002).

The Portal to Texas History. Express Publishing Company, n.d. Accessed September 2, 2016. https://texashistory.unt.edu/ark:/67531/metapth433174/m1/3/?q=cora+clinger.

Chapter 7: Marfa, Texas: Two Gyms for the Price of One

Chinati Foundation | La Fundación Chinati. *Chinati*. Accessed September 18, 2017. www.chinati.org.

Green, Mike. "The History of Hunter Gymnasium." *Big Bend Now*, February 20, 2014, pp. 4–11. Accessed September 18, 2017. bigbendnow.com/2014/02/the-history-of-hunter-gymnasium.

———. Interview with author, July 20, 2008.

"High School Gymnasium—Marfa TX." *Living New Deal*, January 1, 2016. Accessed August 18, 2017. livingnewdeal.org/projects/high-school-gymnasium-marfa-tx.

"Marfa, Texas." *Time Tells*. July 25, 2015. www.visitmarfa.com/arts.php#.Wb_2z7pFxPY.

Ruh, Sarah. "The Arts in Marfa." Visit Marfa, Texas. http://www.visitmarfa.com.

Ulaby, Neda. "Marfa, Texas: An Unlikely Art Oasis in a Desert Town." National Public Radio, August 2, 2012, www.npr.org/2012/08/02/156980469/marfa-texas-an-unlikely-art-oasis-in-a-desert-town.

Chapter 8: Barrio Ball in the Chicken Coop

García, Ignacio M. "An Era Comes to an End, but a School Remains." *When Mexicans Could Play Ball: Basketball, Race, and Identity in San Antonio, 1928–1945*, 218–228. Austin: University of Texas Press, 2013.
———. "Sidney Lanier: An American-Mexican Landscape." In *When Mexicans Could Play Ball*, 89–110.
———. "The Voks Finally Make It to the Top." In *When Mexicans Could Play Ball*, 153–174.
Solis, Manuel. "The Forgotten History of the Mexican-American Team That Ruled Texas HS Basketball In the 1940s." *Remezcla*, August 9, 2016. http://www.remezcla.com/features/sports/forgotten-history-mexican-american-team-ruled-texas-hs-basketball-1940s.

Chapter 9: Heroes of a Small-Town Texas Gym

"Battle of Iwo Jima." History.com. http://www.history.com/topics/world-war-ii/battle-of-iwo-jima.
"Battle of Iwo Jima." ThoughtCo.com. https://www.thoughtco.com/battle-of-iwo-jima-2361486.
"Home Page Set." *Home Page Set*. jacklummus.com.

Chapter 10: Elvis Visits Gyms of Texas

"The Louisiana Hayride Radio Program Premieres on KWKH-AM Shreveport." *History.com*. A&E Television Networks, 2009. Accessed September 23, 2016. http://www.history.com/this-day-in-history/the-louisiana-hayride-radio-program-premieres-on-kwkh-am-shreveport.
Torrance, Lori, and Stanley Oberst. *Elvis in Texas: The Undiscovered King, 1954–1958*. Plano: Republic of Texas, 2002.

Chapter 11: Music in an Old Gym

Bowman, Bob. "Music in an Old Gym." TexasEscapes.com. Texas Escapes LLC. September 13, 2009. Accessed September 23, 2016. http://texasescapes.com/BobBowman/Music-in-an-old-gym.htm.

Chapter 12: Gyms from a Bygone Era: African American Schools and the PVIL

Calvert, Robert A., and Arnoldo De Leon. "Segregation." Texas State Historical Association, June 14, 2010. tshaonline.org/handbook/online/articles/pks01.

McCloud, Lural. Interview with author. June 14, 2006.

McKnight, Roxanne. "Teacher Leaves Eternal Legacy in Changed Lives of Students." *Madisonville Meteor*, July 22, 2008. www.madisonvillemeteor.com/news/article_fb027006-f8f3-518b-b418-bfcad1c77727.html.

"Prairie View Interscholastic League." UIL homepage. www.uiltexas.org/history/pvil.

Chapter 13: A Sad Fate for the Most Beautiful Gym in Texas

"Antelope, Texas." Texas State Historical Association. tshaonline.org/handbook/online/articles/hna35.

Leach, E. "Antelope Gymnasium—Antelope TX." *Living New Deal*, December 30, 2016. livingnewdeal.org/projects/antelope-gymnasium-antelope-tx.

Richards, Lara K. "Faded Glory: Crumbling Antelope Gymnasium Holds Fond Memories." *Times Record News*, January 28, 2008.

Chapter 14: Samnorwood: Where School Was a Family Affair

Anderson, H. Allen. "Samnorwood, TX." Texas State Historical Association. June 14, 2010. tshaonline.org/handbook/online/articles/hls08.

Brown, Clyde Chestnut. "A Survey History of Collingsworth County, Texas." Master's thesis, University of Colorado, 1934.

Oldham, Gary. Interview with author (email). July 17, 2017.

Tarpley, Fred. *1001 Texas Place Names*. Austin: University of Texas Press, 1980.

Chapter 15: Gym Ruins

Dorsey, Bronson. "Scranton." *Lost, Texas,* April 18, 2015. lost-texas. com/2015/04/18/scranton.

"Scranton, Texas." *Texas Escapes.* www.texasescapes.com/TexasTowns/ Scranton-Texas.htm.

Wiggins, Noel. "Scranton, TX." Texas State Historical Association. June 14, 2010. tshaonline.org/handbook/online/articles/hns24.

Chapter 16: Darrouzett: The Town You Can't Get to from Here

Anderson, H. Allen. "Darrouzett, TX." Texas State Historical Association. September 18, 2010. tshaonline.org/handbook/online/articles/hld07.

"Darrouzett, Texas." *Texas Escapes.* www.texasescapes.com/TexasPanhandle Towns/Darrouzett-Texas.htm.

"Lies About Darrouzett." Jokes and Lies. www.jokesandlies.com/7/ txdarrouzett.html.

Chapter 18: Two Magnificent Gyms Still in Use Today

Cottle, Julie Thomas, and Aline Cates McCormack. "Moran School." *Moran School: Past and Present,* 16 Aug. 1999, www.rootsweb.ancestry. com/~txshacke/history.htm.

Edwards, Dean. Interview with author. June 6, 2008.

Hunt, William R. "Morgan Mill, TX." Texas State Historical Association. June 14, 2010. tshaonline.org/handbook/online/articles/hlm87.

Lewis, Lee. Interview with author. August 1, 2016.

"Moran, TX." *The Handbook of Texas Online.* Texas State Historical Association. June 14, 2010. tshaonline.org/handbook/online/articles/hlm85.

Morgan Mill ISD. "History." www.mmisd.us/history.html.

"Morgan Mill, TEXAS." *Texas Escapes.* www.texasescapes.com/ CentralTexasTownsNorth/Morgan-Mill-Texas.htm.

Chapter 19: Activities We Loved in the Old Gym

Kubiak, Len. "Reagan Texas School Campus Tour." Fort Tumbleweed. www.forttumbleweed.net/campus.html.

INDEX

V

van Bruggen, Coosje 49
Vietnam 37

W

Watson, Gene 73
Wells, Kitty 70
*When Mexicans Could Play Ball:
    Basketball, Race, and Identity in
    San Antonio, 1928–1945* 52
Williams, Hank 70
Wills, Bob 70
World War I 86
World War II 19, 46, 88
WPA 17, 18, 19, 20, 31, 46, 48, 86,
    94, 97, 105
W.P. Soash Land Company 21

X

XIT Ranch 21

Z

ZZ Top 72

ABOUT THE AUTHOR

Jackie McBroom describes himself as a "proud native Texan." He grew up in Kennedale, which "used to be a small town" just southeast of Fort Worth. After serving in the U.S. Air Force, he married Sharen Arnold from Orange Grove in 1978.

Jackie coached basketball, football and track, and he taught English at Aubrey High School. He later became the middle school principal at Pilot Point for ten years, and he finished his career as a teacher, principal and assistant superintendent at Sanger ISD. He also served on the Aubrey ISD school board for nine years.

Jackie loves to travel and explore historic sites. During his travels, he continually noticed old school gymnasiums in various states of disrepair, and soon his idea for this book was formed. While he published three articles in various educational journals, *Historic Texas Gyms: A Tribute to Vanishing Traditions* is his first book.

Jackie and Sharen have four boys, Jackie Jr., Kenny, Jesse and Luke; three daughters-in-law, Cindy, Karen and Emily; and five grandkids, Trey, Brody, Chloe, Aubrey and Olivia.

They have loved their home in the country near Aubrey for the last twenty-eight years.

Visit us at
www.historypress.com